TABLE OF CONTENTS

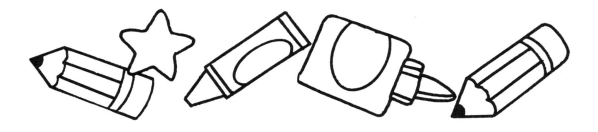

ESSENTIAL SKILLS

Chapter 1   Alphabet Skills
Introduces kindergarten children to the letters and their sounds. This chapter specifically focuses on the sounds the letters make at the beginning of a word. Uppercase and lowercase letters are reinforced. Writing lines are provided to practice letter formation. Open-ended activity pages encourage children to further explore the letters and their sounds.

Chapter 2   Letters & Sounds
Helps kindergartners to recognize and write the letters of the alphabet, both capital and lowercase; to understand that each letter represents a sound; and to hear the sound at the beginning of a word. (At this level, only one sound per letter is presented: the short vowel and the hard consonant.) Children will begin to understand that the sounds of letters blend to form the words they will learn to read and write.

Chapter 3   Numbers 1-10
Helps kindergartners to recognize the numerals 1 to 10, to order them, to understand the counting process, to match and compare sets and to relate them to the correct numeral. These skills develop the strong foundation in math that is essential to later work in addition and subtraction.

Chapter 4   Getting Ready For Reading & Math
Readiness involves all of the child's senses and encompasses many skills. **Getting Ready** reinforces what children learn in kindergarten and prepares them for reading and math. Activities require children to follow directions—an important part of the learning process.

Chapter 5   Reading Readiness
Helps kindergartners build essential pre-reading skills. The book helps children learn to notice and observe things around them. The activities reinforce visual skills such as matching objects, listening skills such as identifying beginning and ending sounds, and reasoning skills such as sequencing events.

Chapter 6   Math Readiness
Reinforces the basic math skills children learn in kindergarten. The activities provide practice in comparing sizes and shapes, completing patterns, counting sets of objects, writing numerals, understanding time and recognizing simple coins. These concepts are essential to developing a strong foundation in math.

Chapter 7   My First Words
Children who are learning to read will benefit from the introduction to sight words and practice provided in **My First Words**. The activities allow children to apply picture clues, context clues and decoding skills as they begin to use their newly acquired words.

How many letters of the alphabet do you know? Say the names of the letters on the alphabet banner. Color the large A.

ABCDEFGHIJK
LMNOPQRST
UVWXYZ

Aa

alligator

 Say the name of each picture. Color the pictures that begin with the same sound as alligator.

astronaut

ant

ball

dog

ambulance

apple

 Trace the letters. Practice printing the letters on the lines.

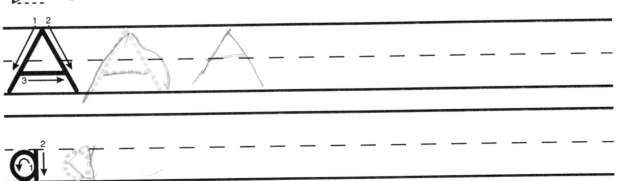

Skill: associating symbols and a sound for the letter A

Color the spaces with the upper or lowercase **Aa** letters in the picture below.

acrobat

Skill: using visual discrimination to identify the letter A

7

Bb

baby

 Say the name of each picture. Draw a line from **Bb** to each picture that begins with the same sound as baby.

baseball

ant

bed

bat

bike

Bb

buttons

apple

 Trace and write.

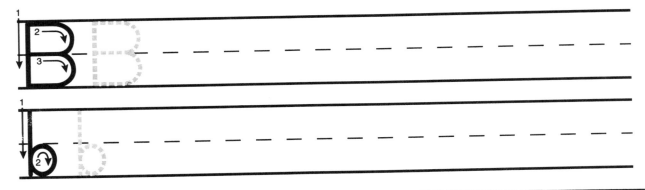

<u>Skill</u>: associating symbols and a sound for the letter B

Banana begins with **Bb**. Draw what you would like to have for breakfast.

Cc

cow

 Say the name of each picture. Draw a circle around the pictures that begin with the same sound as cow.

comb

bed

car

cat

castle

astronaut

Trace and write.

<u>Skill</u>: associating symbols and a sound for the letter C

ALPHABET SKILLS

Follow the path to get the camper to his car.

Dd

dog

 Say the name of each picture. Color the pictures that begin with the same sound as dog.

comb

dinosaur

ball

desk

duck

doctor

Trace and write.

Skill: associating symbols and a sound for the letter D

Say the name of each picture. Draw lines to match the pictures that begin with the same sound.

Skill: matching pictures with the same beginning sound (A-D)

Ee

elephant

 Say the name of each picture. Draw a line from **Ee** to each picture that begins with the same sound as elephant.

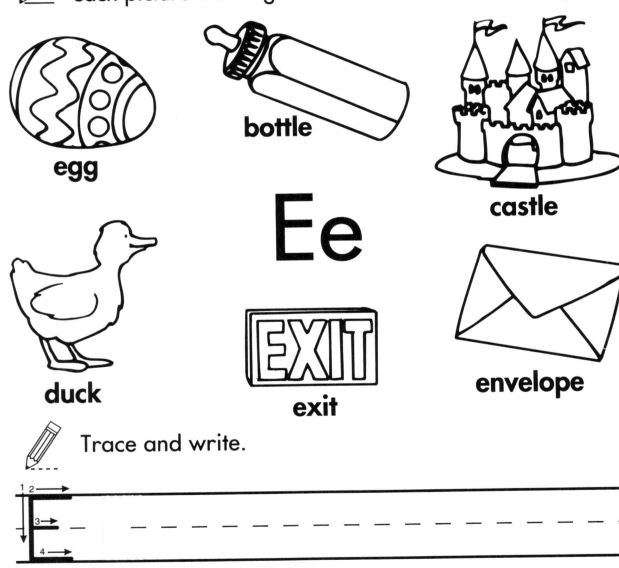

egg

bottle

castle

Ee

duck

EXIT

exit

envelope

 Trace and write.

<u>Skill</u>: associating symbols and a sound for the letter E

Elephant begins with **Ee**. Draw a circus elephant in the picture.

Tell or write about what he is doing.

_____

- - - - - - - - - - - - - - - - - - -

_____

- - - - - - - - - - - - - - - - - - -

_____

Ff

fish

 Say the name of each picture. Draw a circle around the pictures that begin with the same sound as fish.

foot

feather

fork

envelope

dinosaur

Trace and write.

<u>Skill</u>: associating symbols and a sound for the letter F

ALPHABET SKILLS

 Fish begins with **Ff**. Draw fish in the fish tank.

 Name your fish. Tell or write about what they are doing.

_____

– –

_____

– –

_____

Gg

guitar

 Say the name of each object. Color the objects in the picture that begin with the same sound as guitar.

 Trace and write.

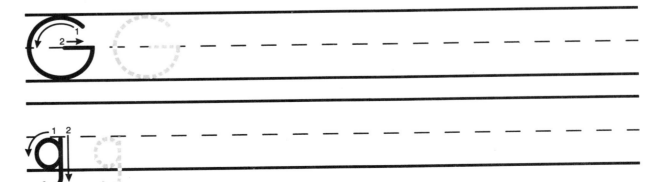

Skill: associating symbols and a sound for the letter G

Color all the upper and lowercase **Gg** letters in the alphabet soup.

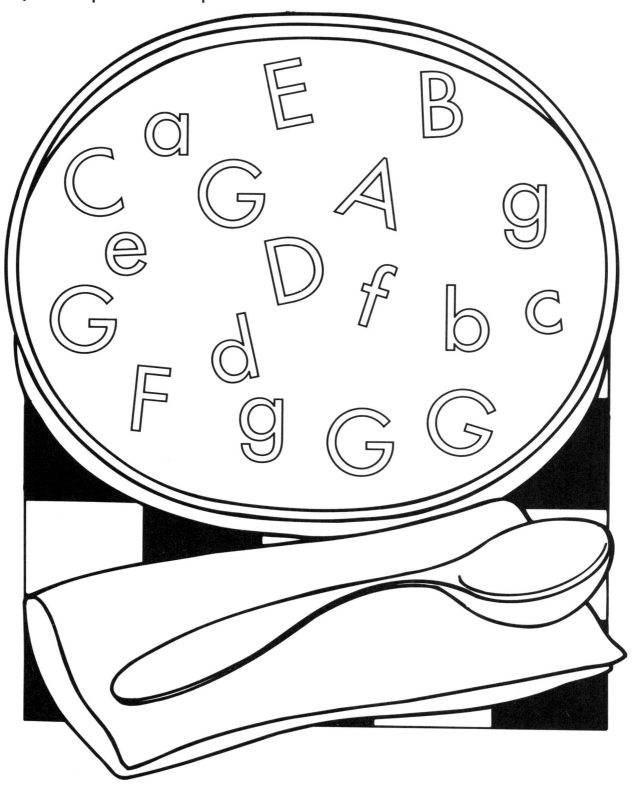

Hh

horse

 Say the name of each picture. Draw a line from **Hh** to each picture that begins with the same sound as horse.

goat

hat

hammer

Hh

feather

heart

helicopter

Trace and write.

<u>Skill</u>: associating symbols and a sound for the letter H

Find and circle the objects in the picture that begin with **Hh**. Draw some hay for the horse to eat.

Ii

igloo

🖍 Say the name of each picture. Color the pictures that begin with the same sound as igloo.

ink

egg

iguana

fish

insect

hammer

✏️ Trace and write.

ALPHABET SKILLS

 Draw a line from each picture to the letter that makes the same beginning sound. Write the upper and lowercase letters that make the beginning sound of the picture that is left.

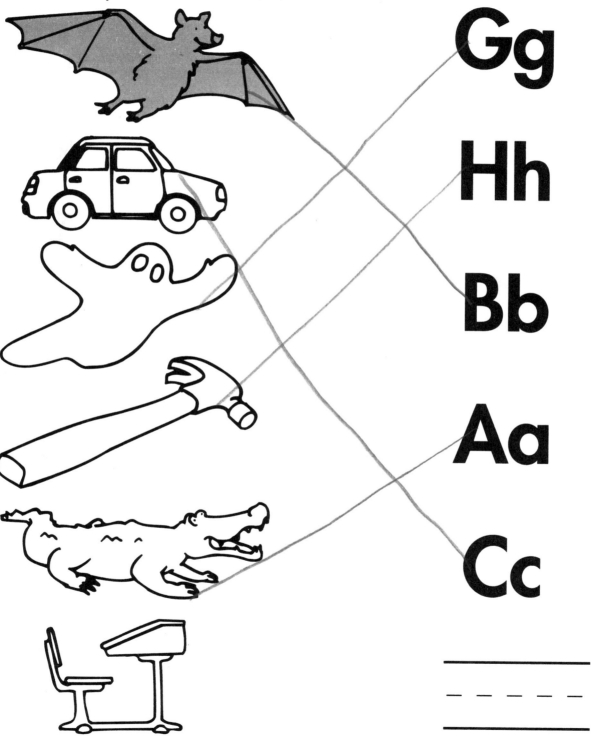

J j

jacket

 Say the name of each picture. Color the pictures that begin with the same sound as jacket.

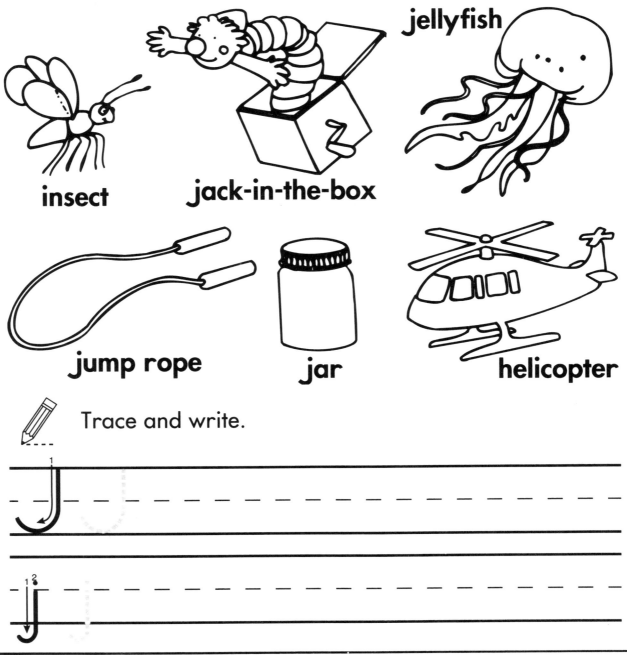

jellyfish

insect

jack-in-the-box

jump rope

jar

helicopter

Trace and write.

<u>Skill</u>: associating symbols and a sound for the letter J

ALPHABET SKILLS

Find and color all the upper and lowercase **Jj** letters that are hidden in the picture.

Kk

kangaroo

 Say the name of each picture. Write the letter for the beginning sound under each picture.

Trace and write.

<u>Skill</u>: associating symbols and a sound for the letter K

Kite begins with **Kk**. Decorate the kite.

Ll

lion

 Find the two lions that are the same. Color them.

Trace and write.

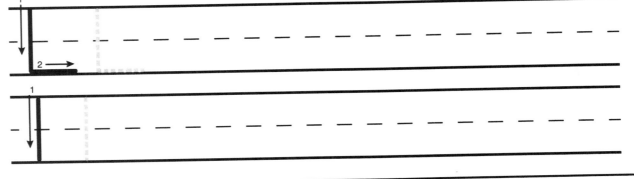

<u>Skill</u>: associating symbols and a sound for the letter L

ALPHABET SKILLS

 Draw lines to match the upper and lowercase letters.

A
B
E
F
H
I
J
L

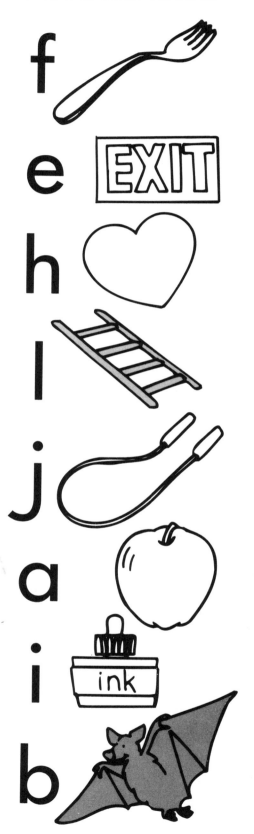

f
e
h
l
j
a
i
b

Mm

monkey

 Say the name of each picture. Write the letter for the beginning sound under each picture.

 Trace and write.

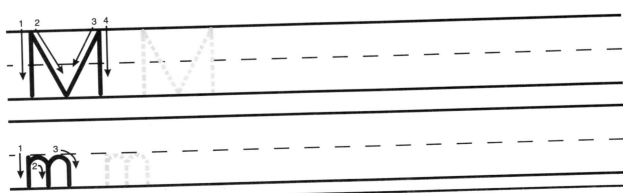

Skill: associating symbols and a sound for the letter M

Mouse Race

You will need: 1 coin, 2 counters (buttons, stones, etc.), and a partner.

Directions: Flip the coin. Heads moves one space; tails moves two spaces. Say the name of the letter you land on. Try to be the first person to get your mouse to the house.

Nn

nickel

 Say the name of each picture. Draw a line from **Nn** to each picture that begins with the same sound as nickel.

nurse

lamp

nut

nail

Nn

mouse

nest

necklace

Trace and write.

Skill: associating symbols and a sound for the letter N

Circle the lowercase letter that matches the uppercase letter.

B h b f g

M e m k d

N f h i n

C c j a l

octopus

 Say the name of each picture. Color the pictures that begin with the same sound as octopus.

monkey

olive

ostrich

otter

octopus

necklace

 Trace and write.

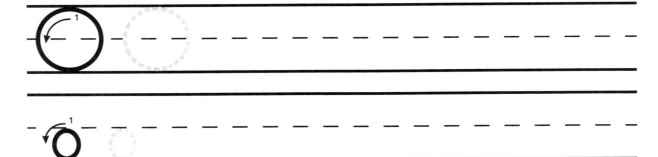

Skill: associating symbols and a sound for the letter O

Color the spaces with the upper or lowercase **Oo** letters in the picture below.

owl

Pp

penguin

 Say the name of each picture. Write the letter for the beginning sound under each picture.

Trace and write.

Skill: associating symbols and a sound for the letter P

Picnic starts with **Pp**. Fill the picnic basket with good things to eat.

<u>Skill</u>: reinforcing the sound for the letter P

Qq

queen

 Say the name of each picture. Draw a circle around the pictures that begin with the same sound as queen.

monkey

quilt

grapes

leaf

quarter

? question mark

quail

Trace and write.

Skill: associating symbols and a sound for the letter Q

Quilt begins with **Qq**. Draw designs to decorate the quilt.

Rr

raccoon

 Say the name of each picture. Draw a line from **Rr** to each picture that begins with the same sound as raccoon.

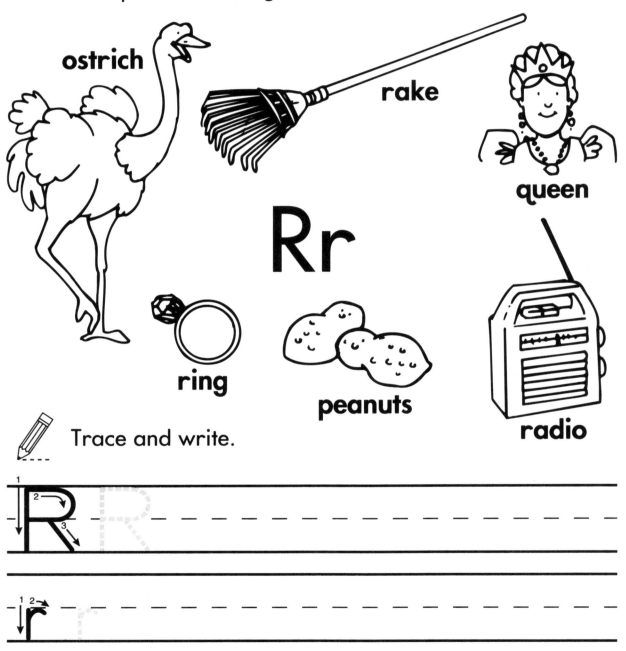

ostrich

rake

queen

Rr

ring

peanuts

radio

 Trace and write.

Skill: associating symbols and a sound for the letter R

Rainbow begins with **Rr**. Color the rainbow. Add things to your picture.

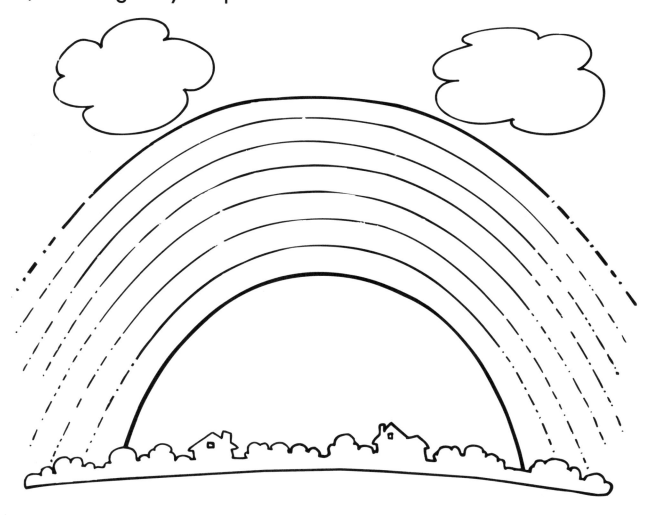

 Tell or write about your picture.

_____

- -

_____

- -

_____

Ss

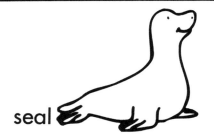

seal

 Say the name of each picture. Draw a line from **Ss** to each picture that begins with the same sound as seal.

quarter

soap

sink

Ss

ring

sun

socks

scissors

 Trace and write.

S

S

Skill: associating symbols and a sound for the letter S

ALPHABET SKILLS

Fill in the uppercase letters that are missing in the snakes.

T t

turtle

 Say the name of each picture. Color the things in the picture that begin with the same sound as turtle.

Trace and write.

<u>Skill</u>: associating symbols and a sound for the letter T

ALPHABET SKILLS

 Add the missing upper and lowercase letters to the train.

Uu

umbrella

 Color the spaces with the upper or lowercase Uu letters in the picture below.

umpire

 Trace and write.

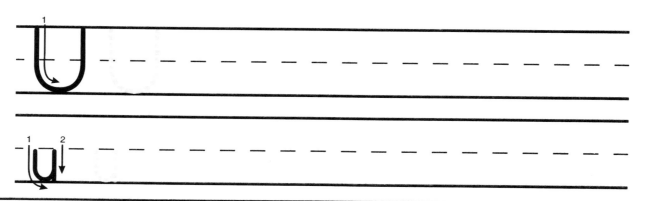

Draw lines to match the upper and lowercase letters.

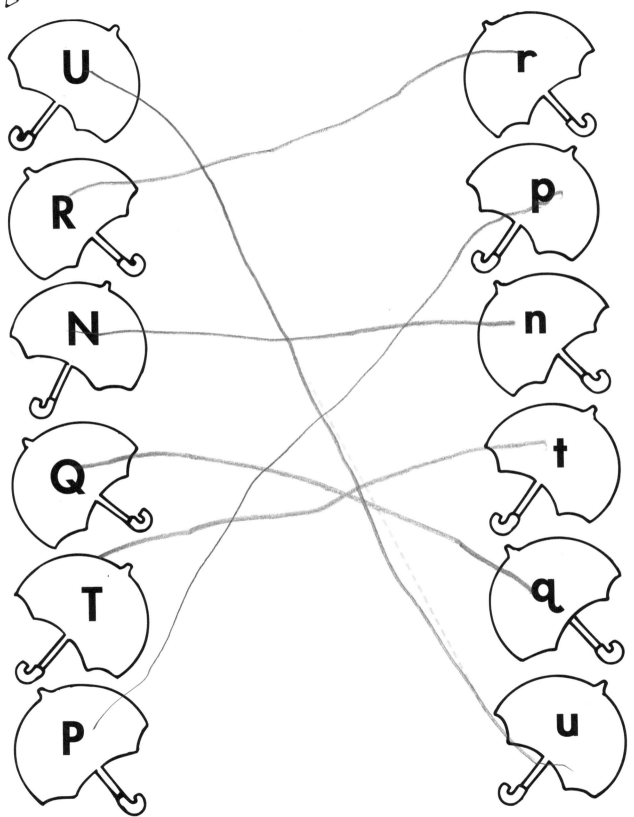

Vv

volcano

 Say the name of each picture. Write the letter for the beginning sound under each picture.

Trace and write.

<u>Skill</u>: associating symbols and a sound for the letter V

Vase begins with **Vv**. Draw some flowers in the vase.

Ww

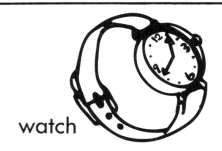
watch

 Say the name of each picture. Draw a circle around the pictures that begin with the same sound as watch.

snowman

witch

violin

web

watermelon

worm

wagon

Trace and write.

Skill: associating symbols and a sound for the letter W

Wagon begins with **Ww**. Fill the wagon with things you like to play with.

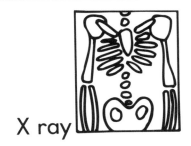

X ray

 Find and color all the upper and lowercase **Xx** letters that are hidden in the picture.

 Trace and write.

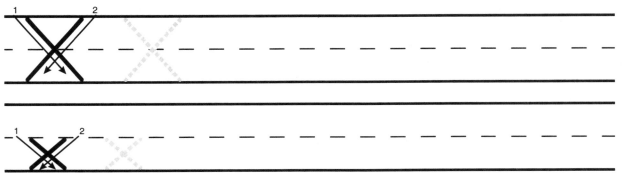

<u>Skill</u>: using visual discrimination to identify the letter X

Race to the Finish

You will need: 1 coin, 2 counters (buttons, stones, etc.), and a partner.

Directions: Flip the coin. Heads moves one space, tails moves two spaces. Say the name of the letter you land on. Try to be the first person to land on X.

 **Yy**

yo-yo

 Color the yak. Draw a yellow flower.

 Trace and write.

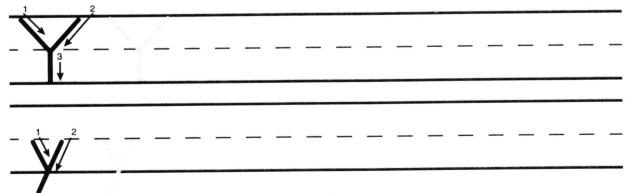

Skill: associating symbols and a sound for the letter Y

Yard begins with **Yy**. Draw a picture of what you play with in your yard.

Zz

zebra

 Say the name of each picture. Color the pictures that begin with the same sound as zebra.

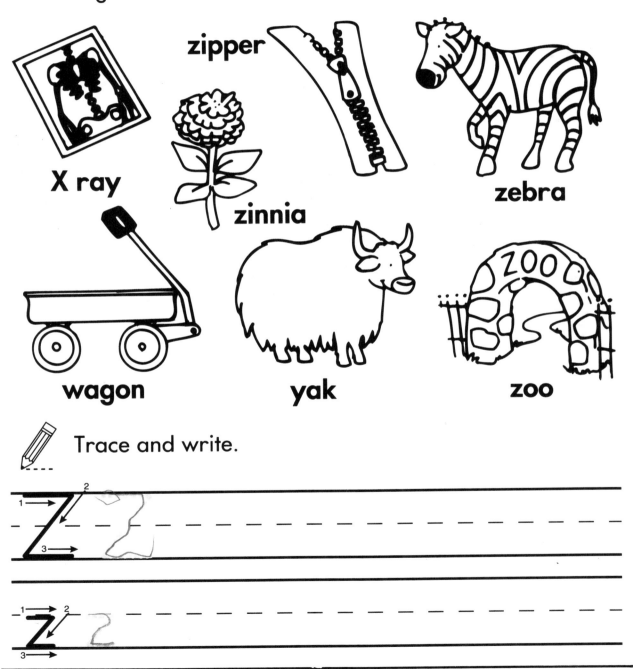

zipper

X ray

zinnia

zebra

wagon

yak

zoo

Trace and write.

Skill: associating symbols and a sound for the letter Z

ALPHABET SKILLS

Connect the letters from A to Z. What do you see?

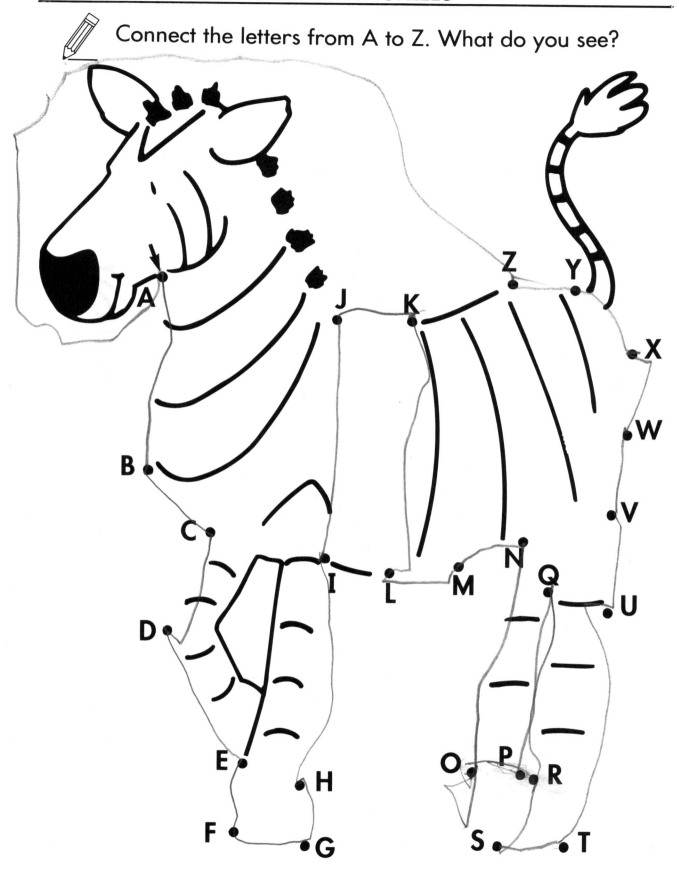

ALPHABET SKILLS

 Draw lines to match the uppercase letters in the butterflies to the lowercase letters in the flowers.

Skill: matching uppercase letters to lowercase letters

Alphabet Puzzles

Cut out all the letter squares on the following pages. Match each uppercase letter with its lowercase letter. Turn the cards over to see something that begins with the same sound.

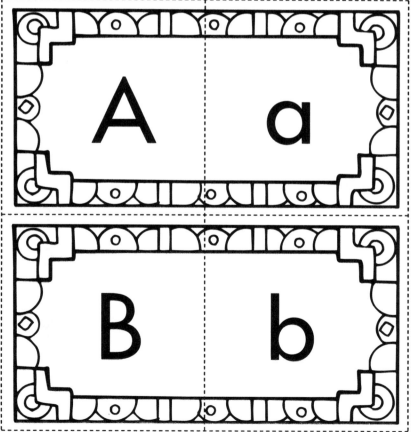

ALPHABET SKILLS

<u>Skill</u>: matching uppercase letters to lowercase letters

Skill: matching uppercase letters to lowercase letters

ALPHABET SKILLS

<u>Skill</u>: matching uppercase letters to lowercase letters

I i

n

J j

N

K k

m

L l

M

Skill: matching uppercase letters to lowercase letters

<u>Skill</u>: matching uppercase letters to lowercase letters

ALPHABET SKILLS

O o   t

P p   T

Q q   s

R r   S

Skill: matching uppercase letters to lowercase letters

65

ALPHABET SKILLS

<u>Skill</u>: matching uppercase letters to lowercase letters

ALPHABET SKILLS

Skill: matching uppercase letters to lowercase letters

67

<u>Skill</u>: matching uppercase letters to lowercase letters

LETTERS & SOUNDS

Look at the picture at the top of each page. Say its name. Listen for the beginning sound.

Aa

 Trace the letters.
Write them on the lines.

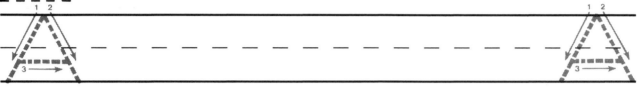

 Say the name of each picture.
Color the pictures that start like apple.

Skill: associating symbols and a sound for the letter A

69

Trace the letters.
Write them on the lines.

Bb

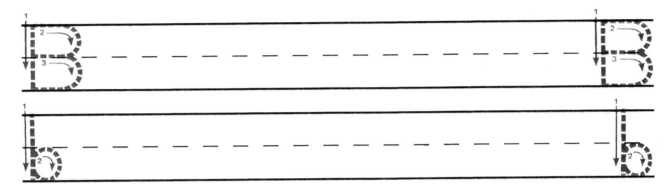

Say the name of each picture.
Color the pictures that start like <u>b</u>all.

<u>Skill</u>: associating symbols and a sound for the letter B

LETTERS & SOUNDS

Trace the letters.
Write them on the lines.

Cc

Say the name of each picture.

Cut and paste the Cc under the pictures that start like cat.

Cc   Cc   Cc

Skill: associating symbols and a sound for the letter C

 Trace the letters.
Write them on the lines.

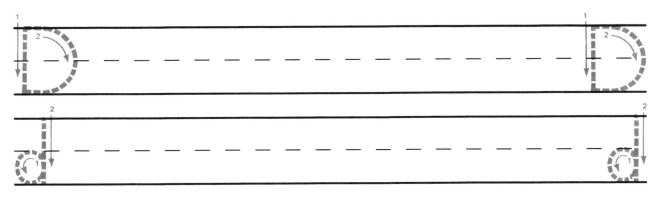

Say the name of each picture.
Draw a line from the $\boxed{Dd}$ to the pictures that
start with <u>Dd</u>.

Skill: associating symbols and a sound for the letter D

LETTERS & SOUNDS

Trace the letters.
Write them on the lines.

Ee

Say the name of each picture.
Color the pictures that start with <u>Ee</u>.

LETTERS & SOUNDS

Trace the letters.
Write them on the lines.

Ff

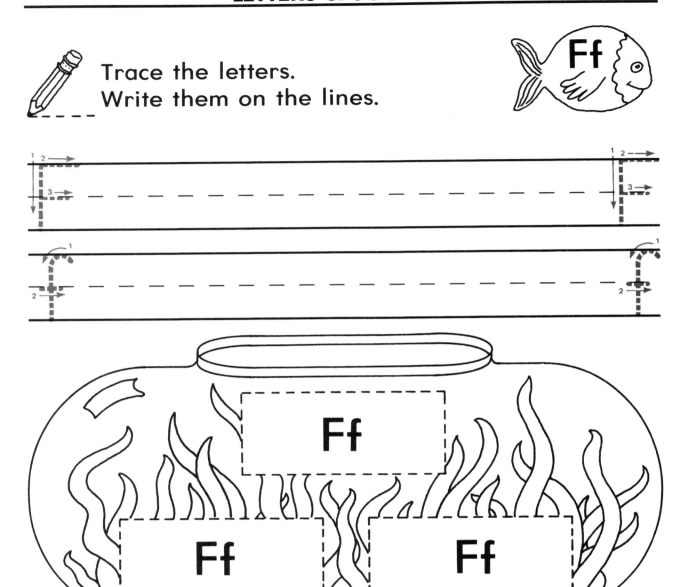

Say the name of each picture. Cut and paste
the pictures that start with **F̲f̲** on the ⌐F̲f̲⌐ spaces.

Skill: associating symbols and a sound for the letter F

LETTERS & SOUNDS

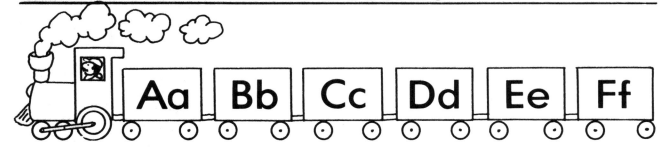

 Say the name of each picture.
Draw a circle around the letter that says the beginning sound.

a b c   c d a   b f e

b d f   c e a   f d e

D A E   F B C   E F D

Skill: reviewing sound and symbol relationships for the letters A-F   75

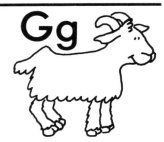

Gg

 Trace the letters.
Write them on the lines.

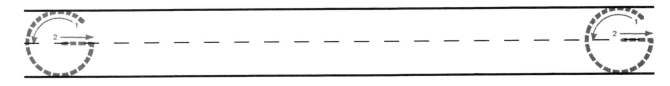

 Say the name of each picture.
Draw a line from the [Gg] to the pictures that
start like goat.

Skill: associating symbols and a sound for the letter G

Trace the letters.
Write them on the lines.

Hh

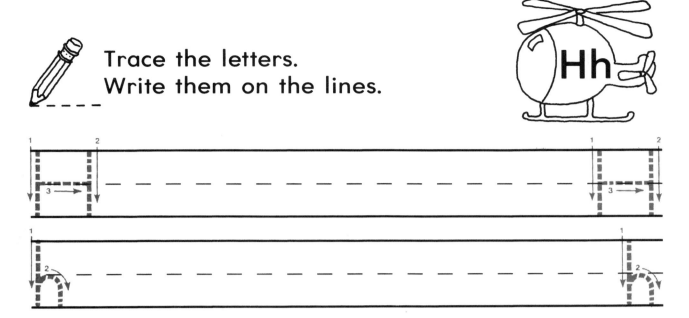

Say the name of each picture.

Color the pictures that start like __h__elicopter.

Trace the letters.
Write them on the lines.

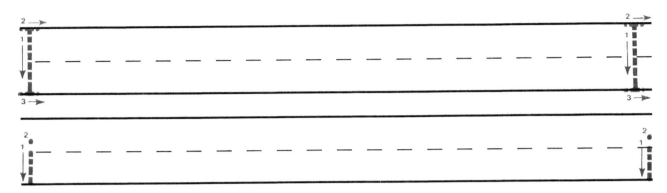

 Follow the letters in order. Start with <u>A</u>.
Draw a line to connect the dots.

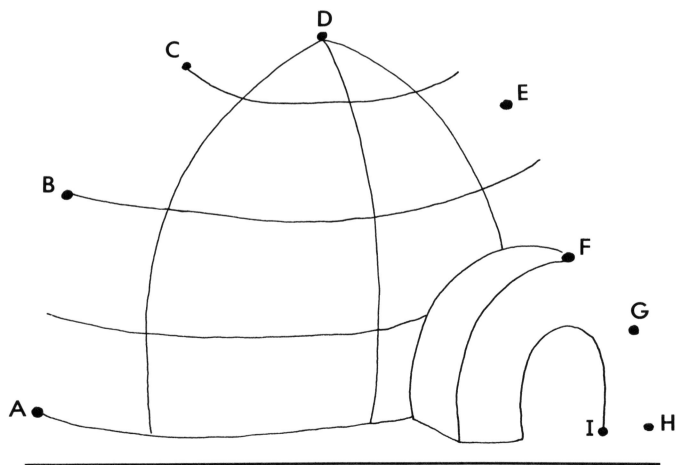

Skill: associating symbols and a sound for the letter I

LETTERS & SOUNDS

 Trace the letters.
Write them on the lines.

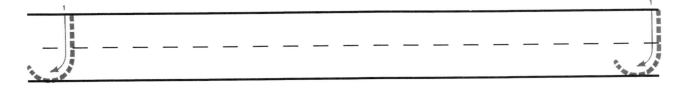

 Say the name of each picture.
Draw a circle around the letter that says the beginning sound.

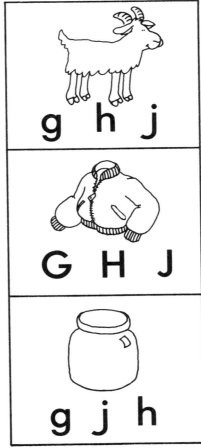

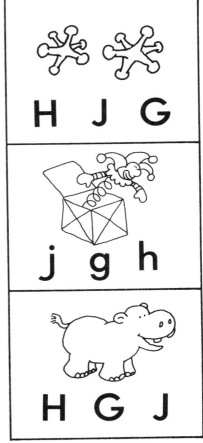

Skill: associating symbols and a sound for the letter J   79

LETTERS & SOUNDS

Trace the letters.
Write them on the lines.

Kk

Trace the letters. Say the name of each picture.
Draw a circle around the picture in each row
that starts with <u>Kk.</u>

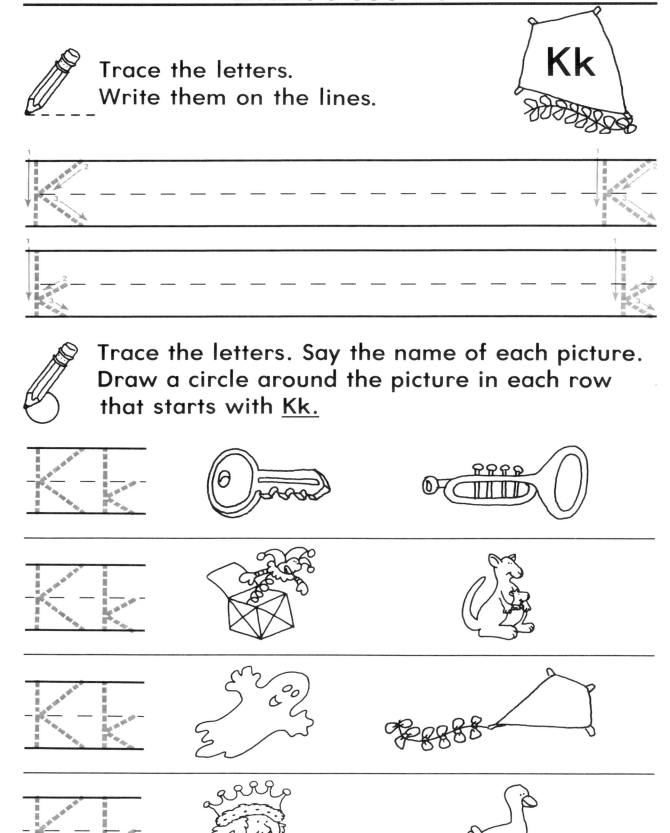

Skill: associating symbols and a sound for the letter K

Ll

Trace the letters.
Write them on the lines.

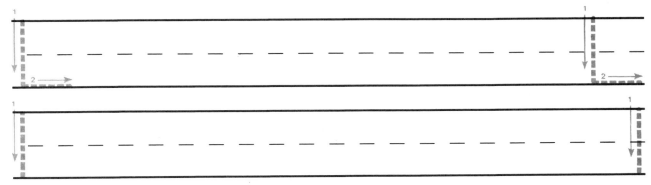

Trace the letters. Say the name of each picture.
Color the picture in each box that starts with <u>Ll</u>.

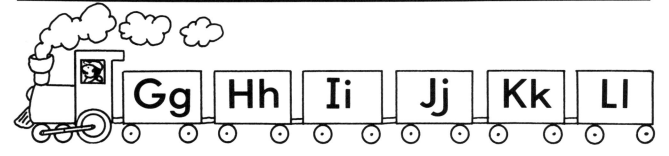

 Look at the letters. Write the small letter on the line next to each capital letter. Draw a line from the letter to the picture with the same beginning sound.

<u>Skill</u>: reviewing sound and symbol relationships for the letters G-L

Mm

 Trace the letters.
Write them on the lines.

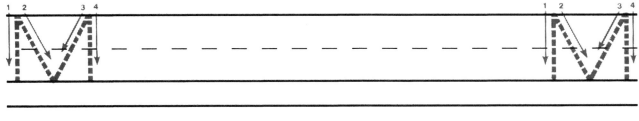

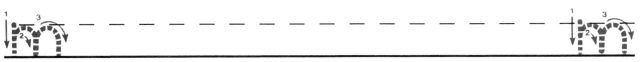

 Draw a line through the path.
Color these pictures that start with <u>Mm</u>.

N n

 Trace the letters.
Write them on the lines.

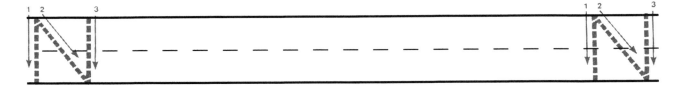

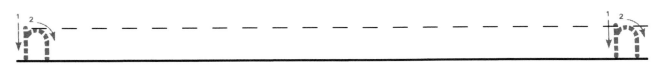

Nn   Nn   Nn

Say the name of each picture. Cut and paste
the pictures that start with Nn on the Nn spaces.

84

Skill: associating symbols and a sound for the letter N

 Trace the letters.
Write them on the lines.

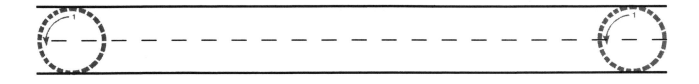

 Follow the letters in order. Start with <u>A</u>.
Draw a line to connect the dots.

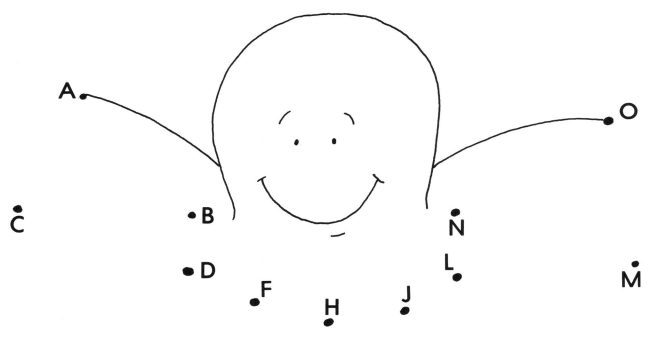

<u>Skill</u>: associating symbols and a sound for the letter O

85

Pp

Trace the letters.
Write them on the lines.

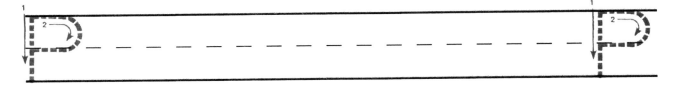

Say the name of each picture.
Color the pictures that start with **Pp**.

86 *Skill:* associating symbols and a sound for the letter P

 Trace the letters.
Write them on the lines.

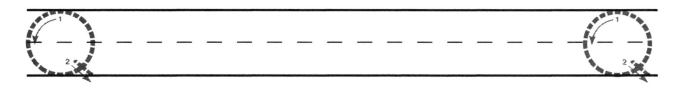

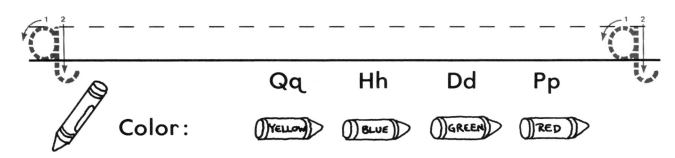

Qq   Hh   Dd   Pp

Color: YELLOW   BLUE   GREEN   RED

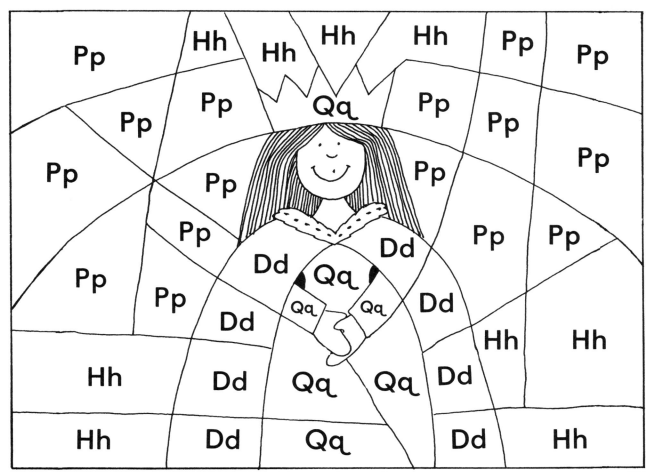

Skill: associating symbols and a sound for the letter Q

LETTERS & SOUNDS

Rr

 Trace the letters.
Write them on the lines.

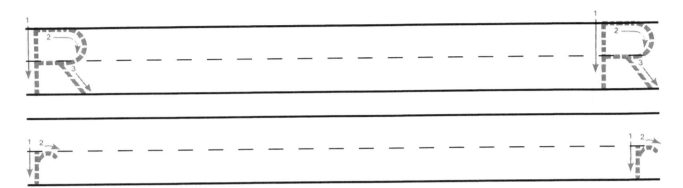

 Say the name of each picture.
Draw a circle around the picture in each box
that starts like <u>r</u>accoon.

<u>Skill</u>: associating symbols and a sound for the letter R

Say the name of each picture.
Draw a circle around the letter that says the beginning sound.

m n o

p q r

q o m

p r n

r n m

q p o

R P Q

N M O

Q O P

Skill: reviewing sound and symbol relationships for the letters M-R

Trace the letters.
Write them on the lines.

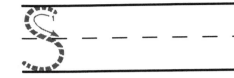

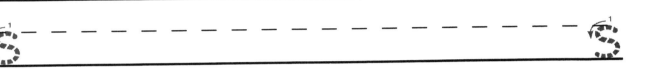

 Say the name of each picture. Draw a circle around the pictures that start like <u>sun</u>.

<u>Skill</u>: associating symbols and a sound for the letter S

Trace the letters.
Write them on the lines.

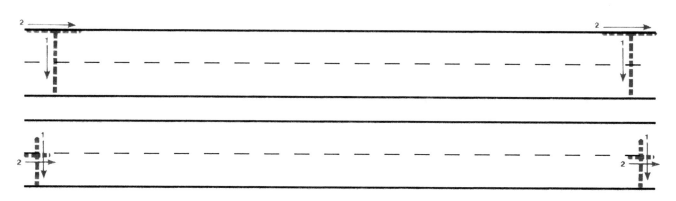

 Trace the letters. Say the name of each picture.
Draw a circle around the pictures in each row
that start with <u>Tt</u>.

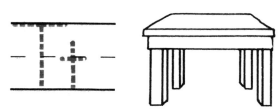

<u>Skill</u>: associating symbols and a sound for the letter T

Trace the letters.
Write them on the lines.

 Uu

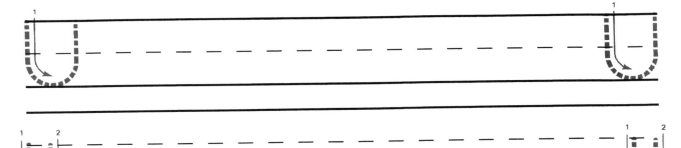

 Follow the letters in order. Start with <u>A</u>.
Draw a line to connect the dots.

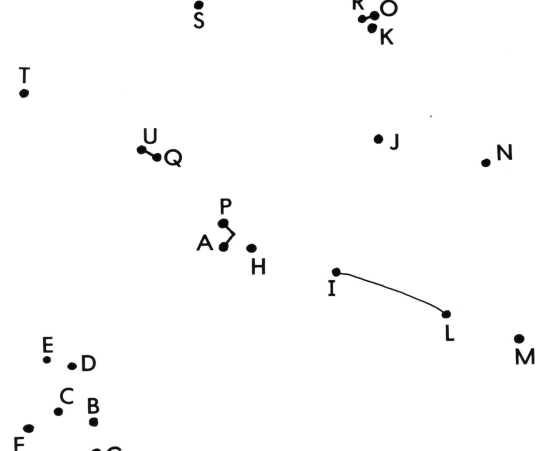

Skill: associating symbols and a sound for the letter U

Trace the letters.
Write them on the lines.

Vv

Color the valentine.

V ()red)   S ()yellow)   T ()blue)

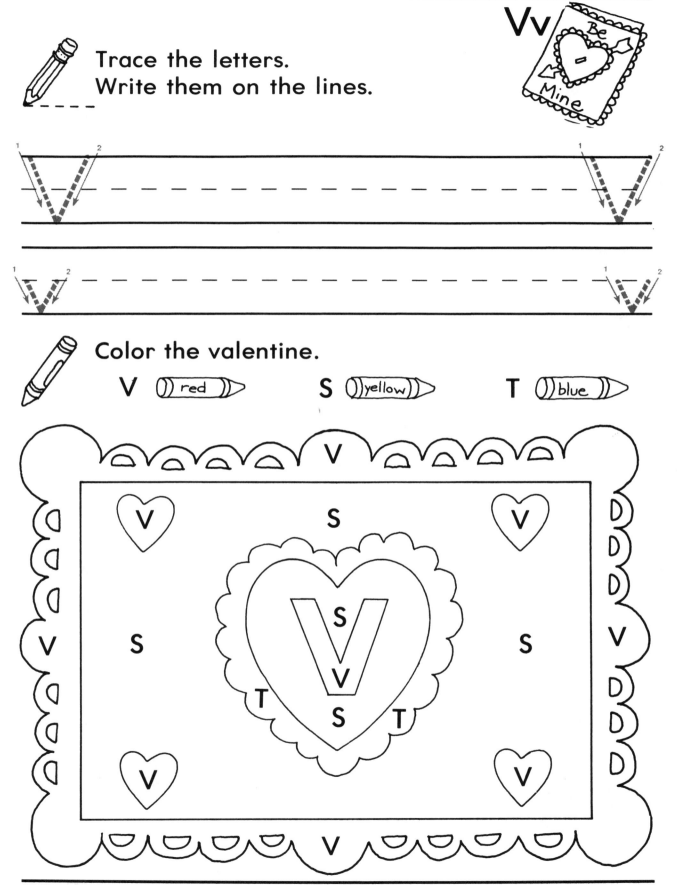

W w

Trace the letters.
Write them on the lines.

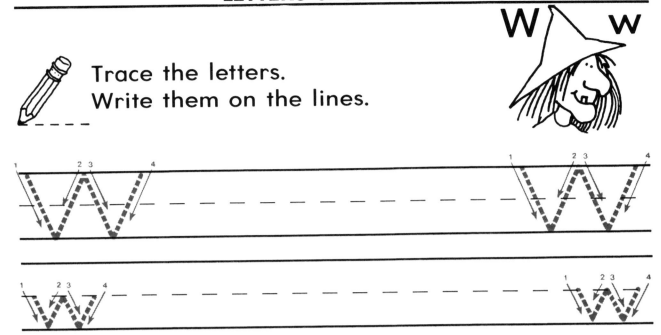

Say the name of each picture.

Color the pictures that start like <u>w</u>itch.

<u>Skill</u>: associating symbols and a sound for the letter W

X 😊 x

Trace the letters.
Write them on the lines.

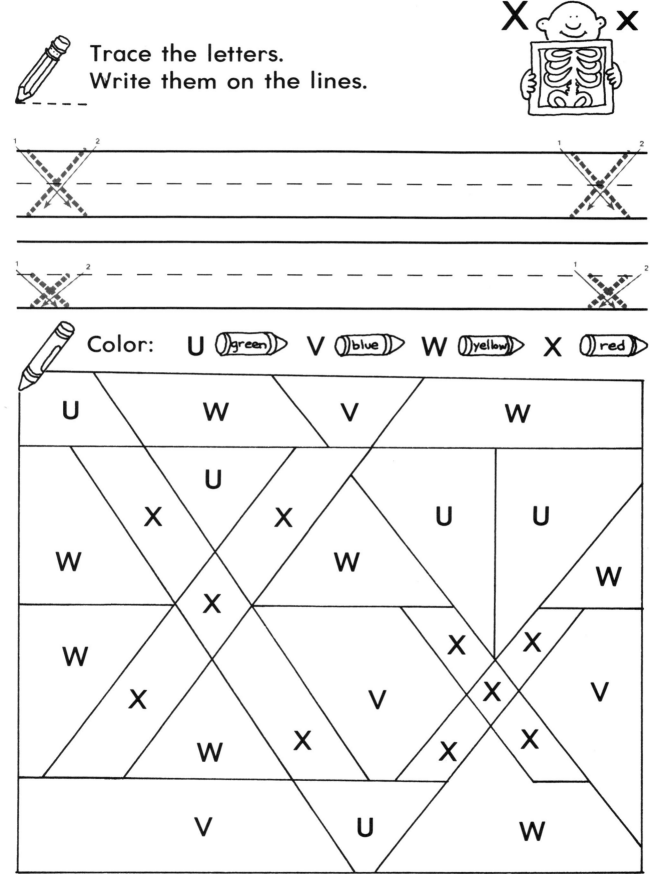

Color: U 🖍green V 🖍blue W 🖍yellow X 🖍red

Skill: associating symbols and a sound for the letter X

 Look at the letters. Write the small letter on the line next to each capital letter. Draw a line from the letter to the picture with the same beginning sound.

Skill: reviewing sound and symbol relationships for the letters S–X

LETTERS & SOUNDS

 Trace the letters.
Write them on the lines.

 Say the name of each picture.
Draw a circle around the letter that says the beginning sound.

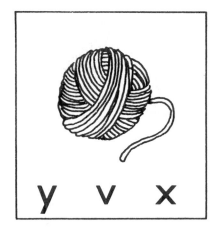

y   v   x

w   v   y

t   y   v

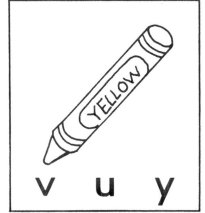

v   u   y

y   t   x

u   y   v

Skill: associating symbols and a sound for the letter Y

97

LETTERS & SOUNDS

 Trace the letters.
Write them on the lines.

Zz

 Say the name of each picture.
Draw a line from the Zz to the pictures that start with Zz.

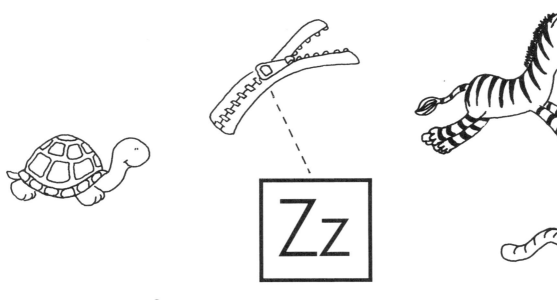

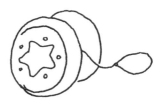

Skill: associating symbols and a sound for the letter Z

LETTERS & SOUNDS

Write the missing letters.

LETTERS & SOUNDS

Write the missing letters.

Mm | ___ | Oo

___ | Qq | ___

Ss | Tt | ___

Vv | ___ | Xx

___ | Zz | The end!

<u>Skill</u>: sequencing letters of the alphabet; writing capital and lowercase letters

Review

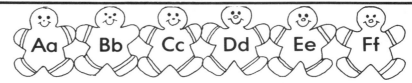

Aa Bb Cc Dd Ee Ff

 Trace the letters. Draw a circle around the picture in each box that begins with the same sound.

Skill: reviewing sound and symbol relationships for the letters A-F

101

Review

Gg Hh Ii Jj Kk Ll

 Say the name of each picture. Draw a circle around the letter that says the beginning sound.

J **G** L

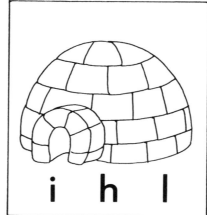

i h l

L H K

i k h

j g h

L K G

l k i

H K I

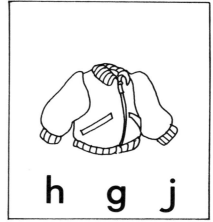

h g j

102   <u>Skill</u>: reviewing sound and symbol relationships for the letters G-L

Review

 Say the name of each picture.
Draw a circle around the letter that says the beginning sound.

Mm   **Nn**

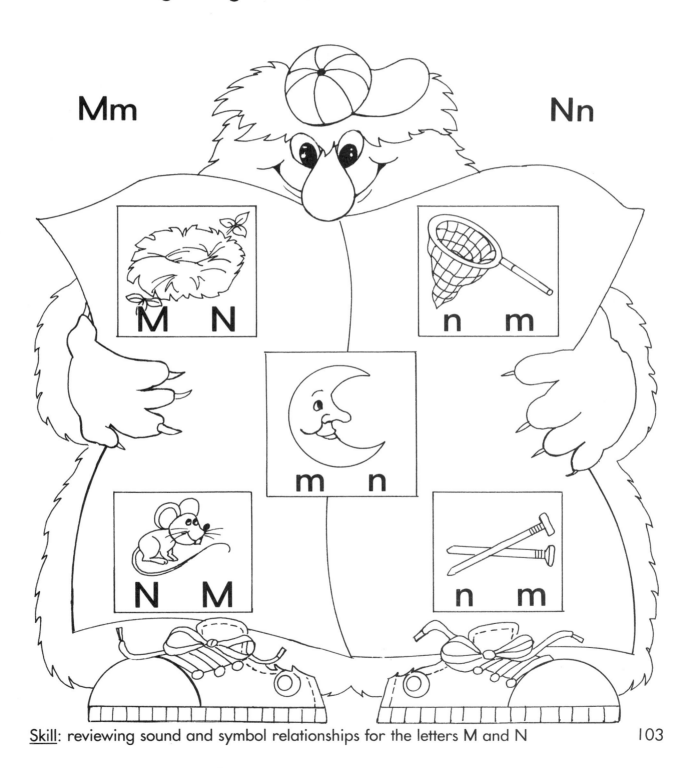

M   N

n   m

m   n

N   M

n   m

Skill: reviewing sound and symbol relationships for the letters M and N   103

Review

Aa Ee Ii Oo Uu

Aa Ee Ii Oo Uu

 Say the name of each picture. Trace the capital letters. Write the small letters. Then color the pictures.

Skill: reviewing sound and symbol relationships for the vowels; A-E-I-O-U

Review

Say the name of each picture.
Put an X on things that start with Y.
Put a O around things that start with W.

Say the name of each picture.
Draw a circle around the letter that says
the beginning sound.

w y

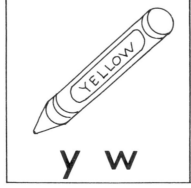

y w

W Y

Skill: reviewing sound and symbol relationships for the letters W and Y

Review

Write the small letter for each capital letter.

A B C D E

F G H I J

K M M N O

P Q R S T

U V W X Y

Z

Skill: sequencing the letters of the alphabet; writing lowercase letters

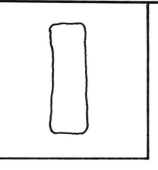

one

Trace the number. Write it on the line.

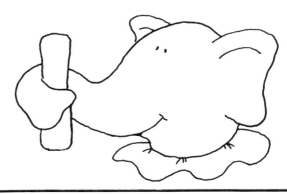

Skill: recognizing and writing the numeral 1; counting one object

2

two

Trace the number. Write it on the line.

2 2   2

2 ☆
  ☆

Skill: recognizing and writing the numeral 2; counting two objects

three

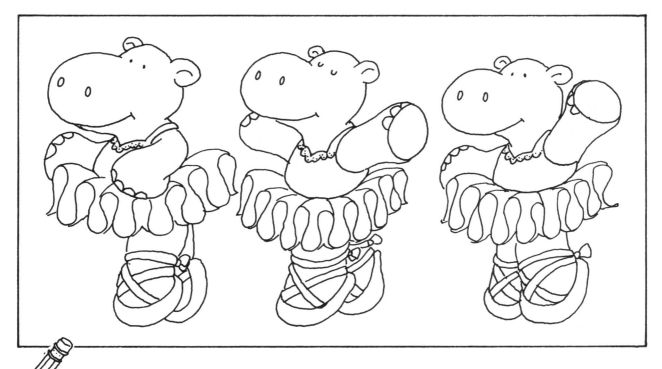

Trace the number. Write it on the line.

3 3 - - - - - - - - - - - - 3

Skill: recognizing and writing the numeral 3; counting three objects

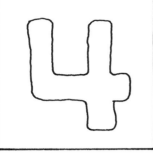 **four**

Trace the number. Write it on the line.

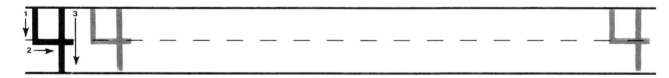

<u>Skill</u>: recognizing and writing the numeral 4; counting four objects

5

five

Trace the number. Write it on the line.

5 5

Skill: recognizing and writing the numeral 5; counting five objects

111

NUMBERS 1-10

Count the objects in each set.
Trace the numbers.

Skill: recognizing and tracing the numerals 1-5

Matching

Draw a line from the 2 to the sets with 2 ☆.

Draw a line from the 5 to the sets with 5 🌙.

Skill: matching a numeral to sets with the same number of members

Count the objects in each set.
Draw a circle around the right number.

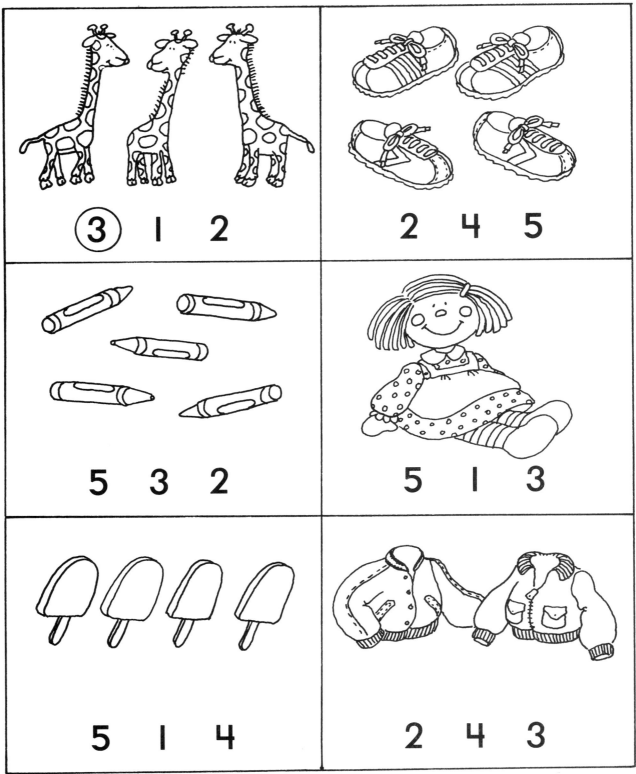

(3)   1   2   2   4   5

5   3   2   5   1   3

5   1   4   2   4   3

<u>Skill</u>: matching the number of members in a set to the correct numeral

six

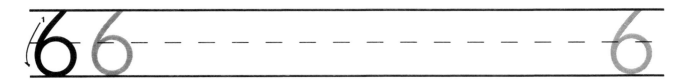

Trace the number. Write it on the line.

Skill: recognizing and writing the numeral 6; counting six objects

 **seven**

Trace the number. Write it on the line.

Skill: recognizing and writing the numeral 7; counting seven objects

NUMBERS 1-10

Count the animals in each set.

 Cut and paste the right number next to each set of animals.

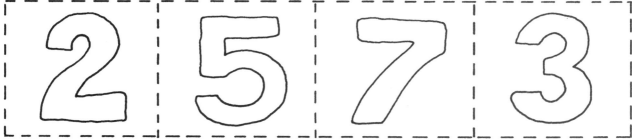

NUMBERS 1-10

Look at the circus pictures. Color them.

Count the animals. Write the number.

How many 🦭 ? [— — —]   How many 🐴 ? [— — —]

How many 🦁 ? [— — —]   How many ⚽ ? [— — —]

NUMBERS 1-10

 Look at the number. Count the objects.
Color the right number of objects
in each set.

NUMBERS 1-10

 Count the objects in each set.
Trace the right number.

3 2 5 4

8 6 5 9

2 4 1 7

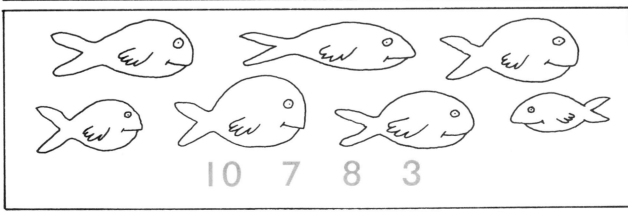

10 7 8 3

Skill: matching the number of members in a set to the correct numeral

eight

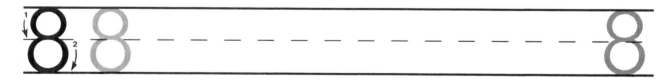

Trace the number. Write it on the line.

8 8 ------- 8

Skill: recognizing and writing the numeral 8; counting eight objects

NUMBERS 1-10

 Count the animals in each set.
Write the number on the line.

How many?

_____
- - - - - -
_____

How many?

_____
- - - - - -
_____

How many?

_____
- - - - - -
_____

Skill: counting the members in a set and writing the correct numeral

Count the objects in each set.
Write the number on the line.

How many?

_____

— — — — —

_____

How many?

_____

— — — — —

_____

How many?

_____

— — — — —

_____

How many?

_____

— — — — —

_____

Matching

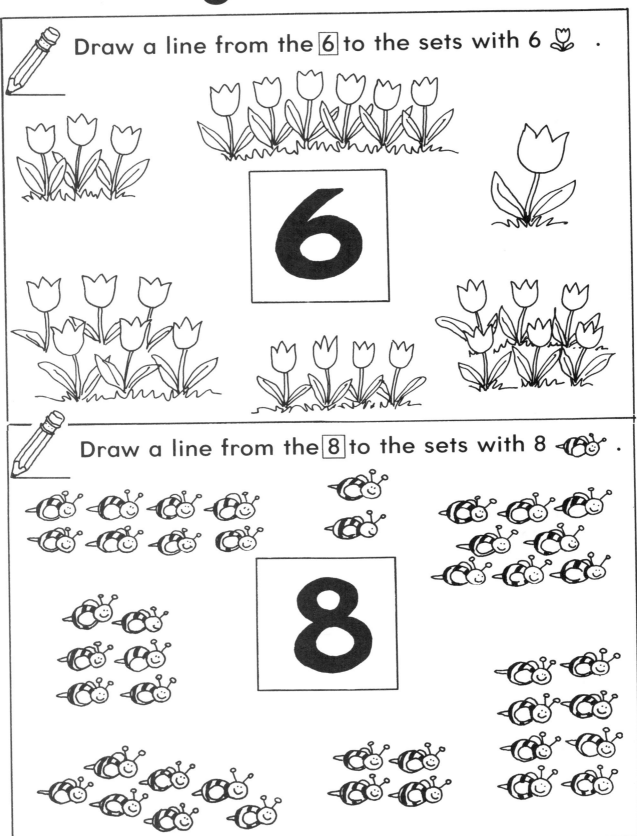

Draw a line from the 6 to the sets with 6 🌷 .

6

Draw a line from the 8 to the sets with 8 🐝 .

8

<u>Skill</u>: matching a numeral to sets with the same number of members

9

nine

Trace the number. Write it on the line.

Skill: recognizing and writing the numeral **9**; counting nine objects

ten

Trace the number. Write it on the line.

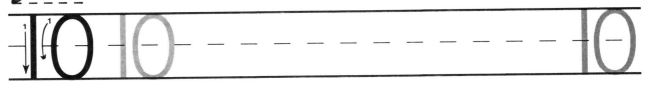

<u>Skill</u>: recognizing and writing the numeral 10; counting ten objects

NUMBERS 1-10

 Count the objects in each set.
Write the number on the line.

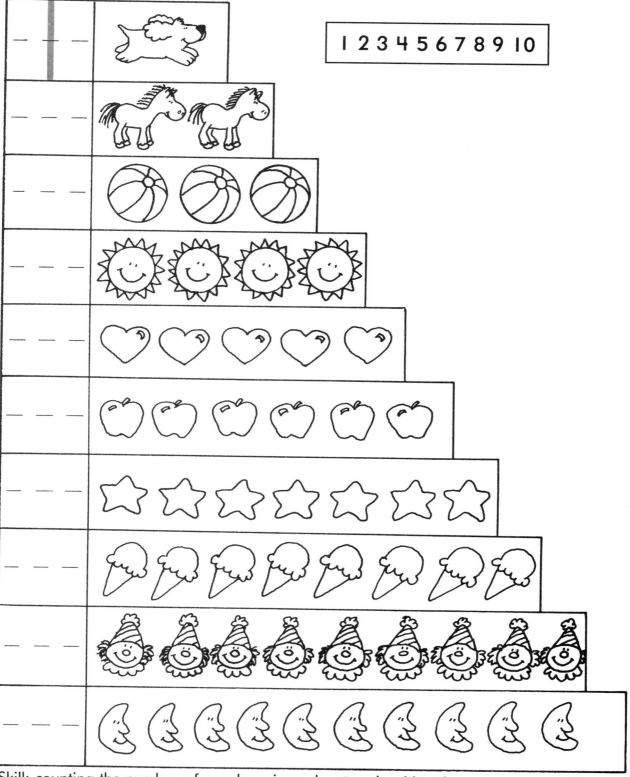

1 2 3 4 5 6 7 8 9 10

NUMBERS 1-10

 Look at the number. Count the objects.
Color the right number of objects in each set.

color

9

color

7

color

10

color

8

Skill: coloring the correct number of members to complete a specific set

NUMBERS 1-10

Write the missing numbers on the lines.

1 2 3 4 5 6 7 8 9 10

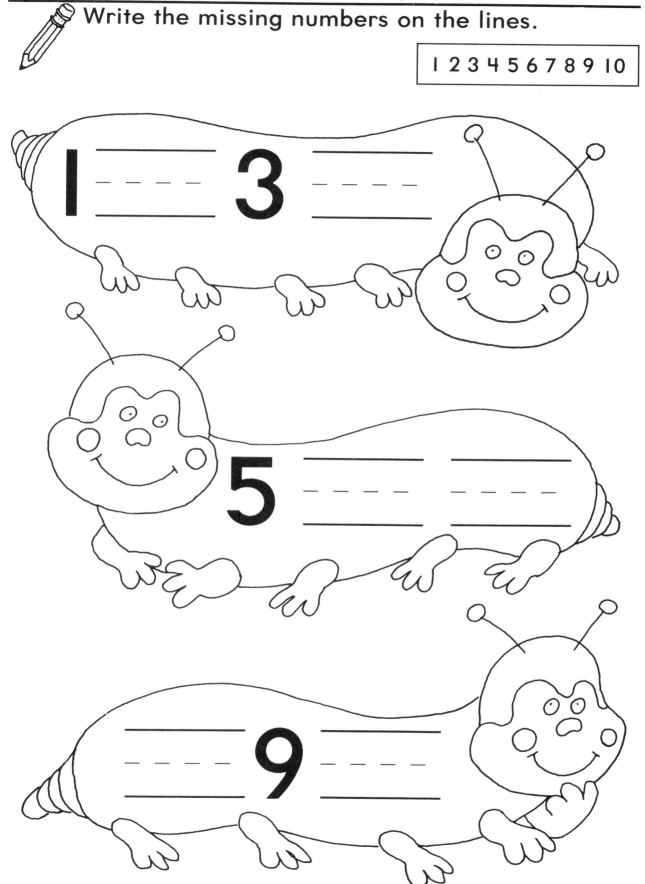

NUMBERS 1-10

 Count the objects in each set.
Draw a circle around the right number.

Skill: matching the number of members in a set to the correct numeral

Matching

Draw a line from each number to the set with the same number of objects.

| 6 |
| 2 |
| 10 |
| 1 |
| 4 |
| 5 |

NUMBERS 1-10

 Count the objects in each set.
Write the number on the line.

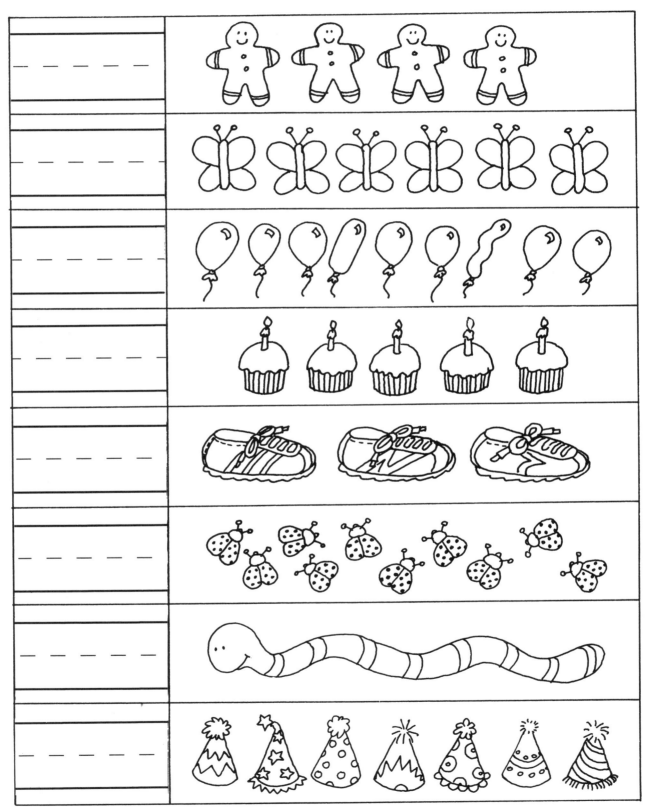

Skill: counting the members of a set and writing the correct numeral

NUMBERS 1-10

Start at 1. Count the numbers in order to 10.
Draw a line to connect the dots.

7
•

6 •

• 8

Dusty

3 •

• 2

5 •

4 •

I
•
10

• 9

Find the numbers hidden in the picture.
Draw a circle around them.

<u>Skill</u>: recognizing the numerals 1-10

NUMBERS 1-10

Write the missing numbers on the lines.

countdown

10

7

6

3

1

BLAST OFF!

Hidden Picture

 Count the dots. Find the number.
Color the picture.

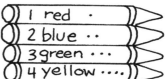

| 1 red · |
| 2 blue ·· |
| 3 green ··· |
| 4 yellow ···· |

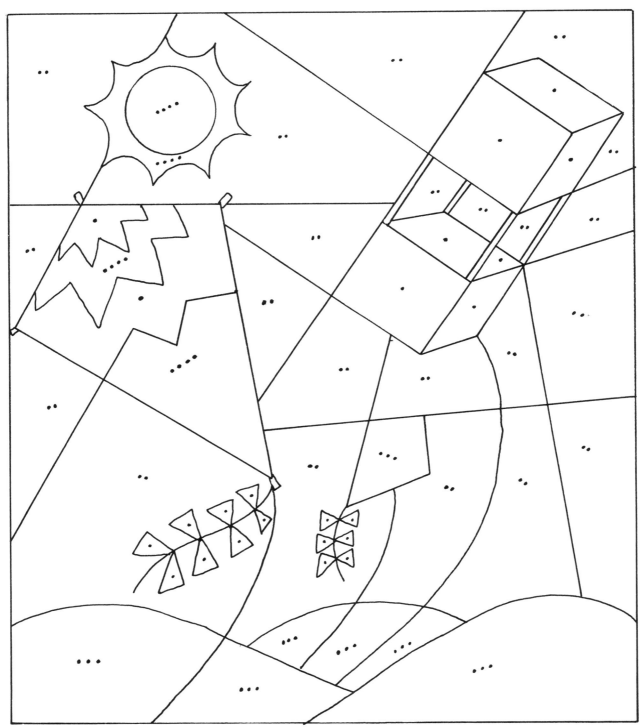

136

<u>Skill</u>: completing a picture by using a color code

Shapes

Look at the shapes.

Trace the line around each shape to complete it.

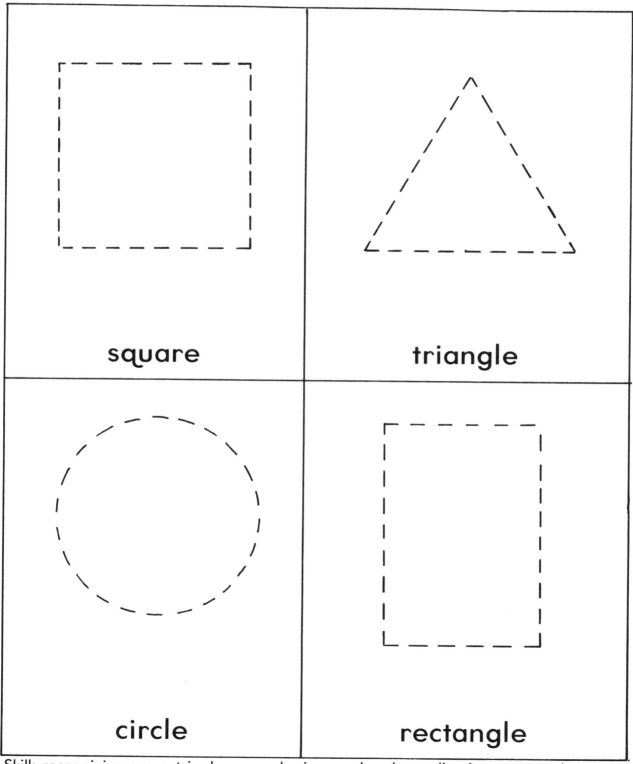

square

triangle

circle

rectangle

Match the Shapes

 Color the shape in each row that matches the shape in the box.

<u>Skill</u>: finding the matching shapes

Find the Shapes

Find the hidden shapes in the picture.

Color the △ 's blue.

Color the ◯ 's red.

Color the ▢ 's yellow.

Color the ▭ 's green.

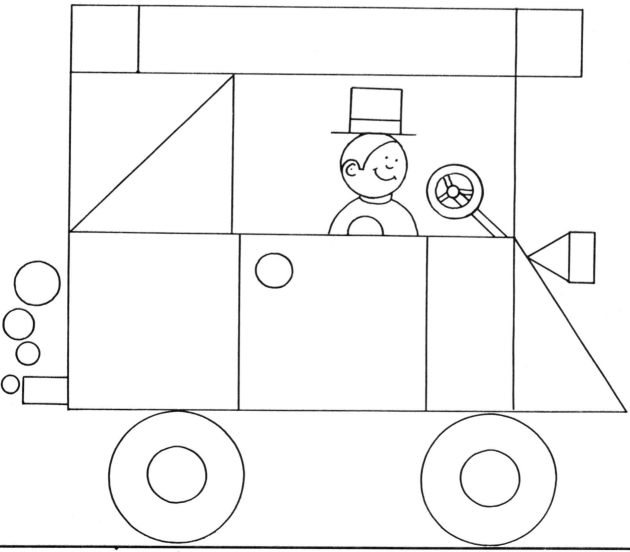

Paths

 Trace the paths.

<u>Skill</u>: using eye-hand coordination to trace left to right patterns

Color Words

 Color the picture.

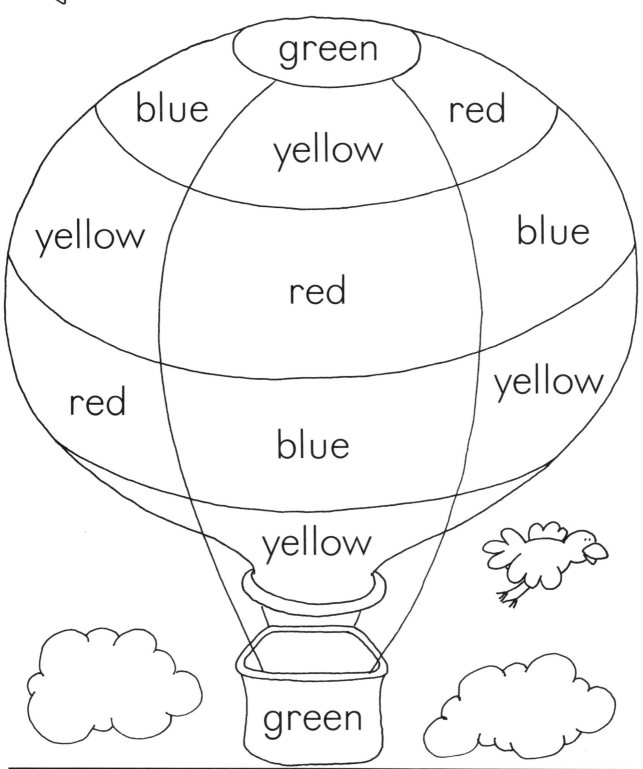

Small

Look at the picture.
Color the bunny that is the **smallest**.

<u>Skill</u>: making perceptual comparisons

Small—Smaller—Smallest

Look at the pictures.
Color the **smallest** bug in each box .

<u>Skill</u>: making perceptual comparisons

143

Big

Look at the picture.
Color the dog that is the **biggest**.

Skill: making perceptual comparisons

Big—Bigger—Biggest

Each dog at the bottom of the page is a different size.

 Find the dog that fits each doghouse.
Cut out the dog and paste it where it belongs.

Skill: making perceptual comparisons   145

Maze Fun

Follow the path. Draw a line from the 🤡 to his 🚗.

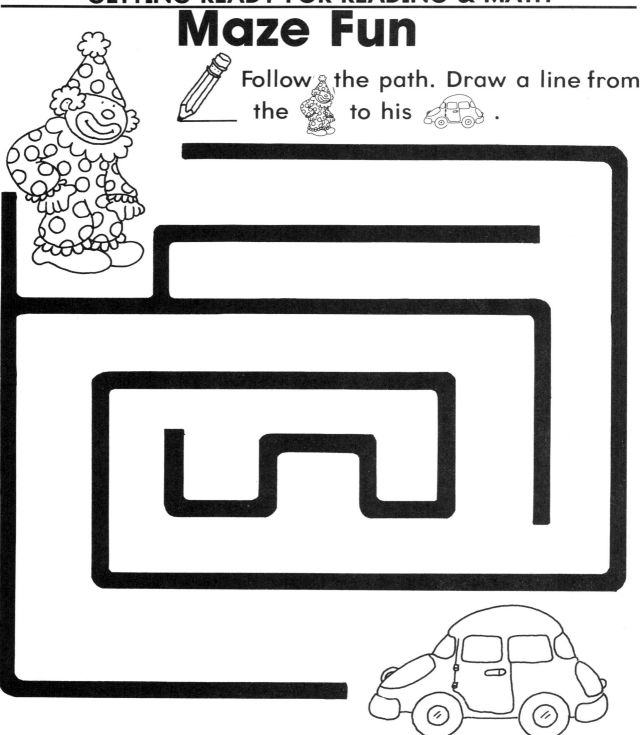

Same

 Look at the pictures in each row.
Draw a circle around the picture that is the
same as the picture in the box.

<u>Skill</u>: using visual discrimination to match pictures

Different

Look at the pictures.
Color the one that is **different**.

<u>Skill</u>: using visual discrimination to identify the picture that is different

Different

Look at the pictures in each row.
Draw a circle around the one that is **different**.

Skill: using visual discrimination to identify the picture that is different

Dot to Dot

Start with the letter __A__. Follow the letters in order. Draw a line to connect the dots.

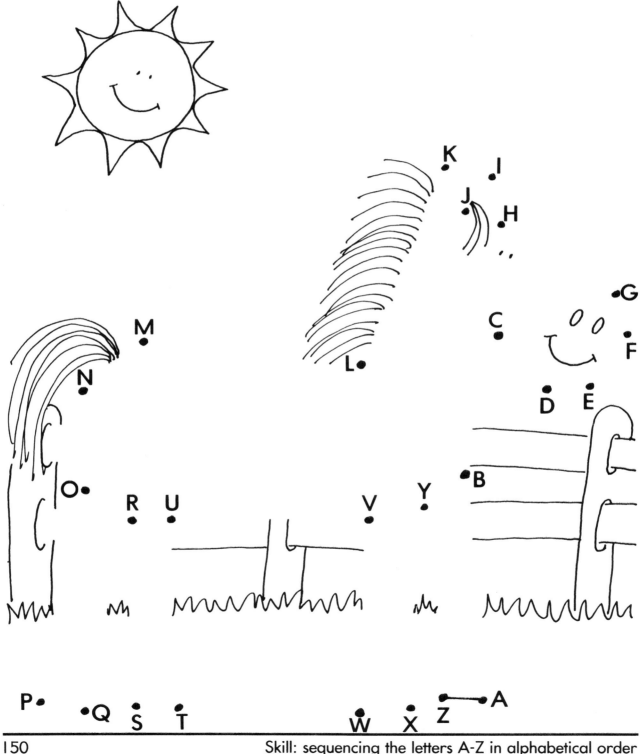

<u>Skill</u>: sequencing the letters A-Z in alphabetical order

Pairs

Look at the pictures. Make a pair.
Draw a circle around the picture in each row
that makes a pair with the picture in the box.

Skill: using visual discrimination to match pairs of object

Things that Go Together

Look at the pictures in the box.
Draw a circle around the two pictures in each row
that go with the pictures in the box.

Skill: using visual discrimination to classify objects with common attributes

Things that Go Together

 Look at the pictures. Draw a line from the objects to the right picture.

Homes

 Draw a line from each animal to its home.

Skill: understanding the relationship of an animal to its home

Missing Parts

Draw the missing parts.

Matching

 Draw a line to match the objects.

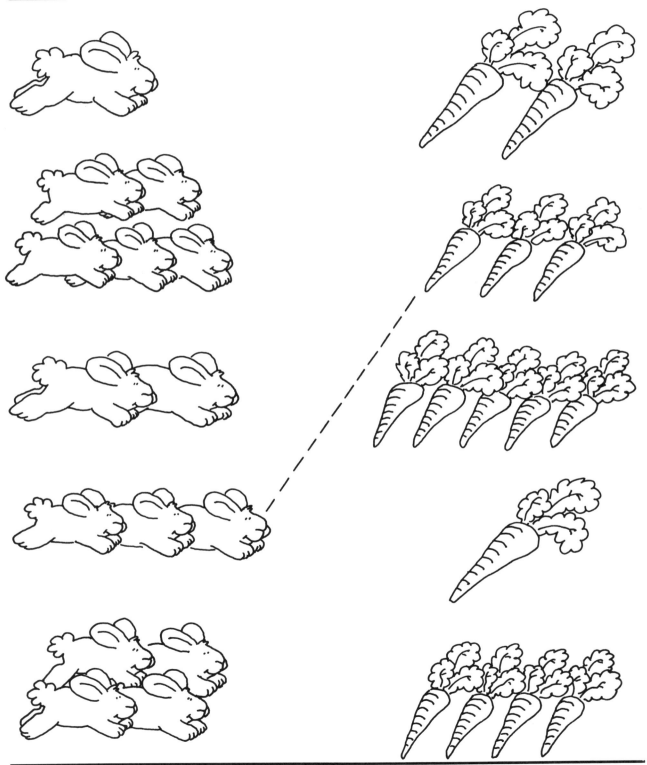

<u>Skill</u>: using 1 to 1 correspondence to match sets

Dot to Dot

Start with <u>1</u>. Follow the numbers in order to 10.
Draw a line to connect the dots.

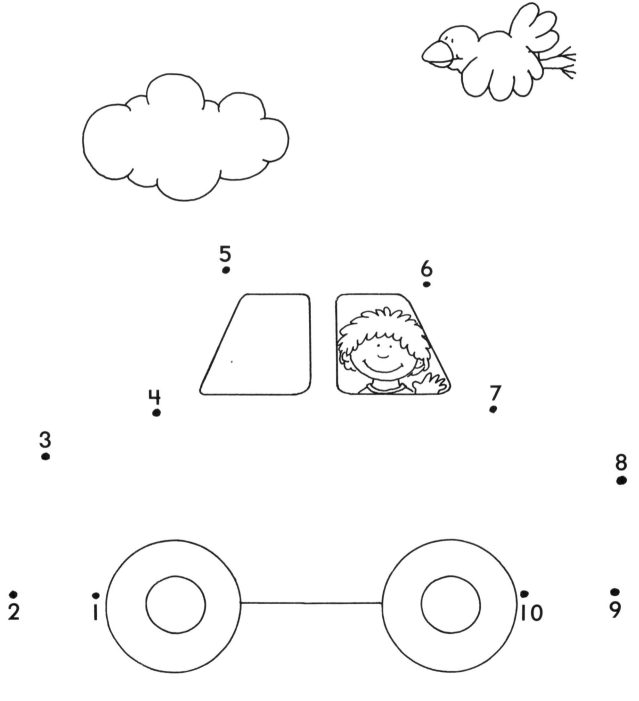

Patterns

Finish the patterns. What comes next?

△ ○ △ ○ △

✂ Cut and paste the ⬚ where they belong to finish the patterns.

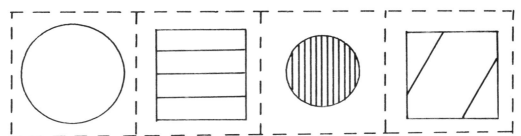

158   Skill: using visual discrimination to complete patterns

Rhyming Pictures

 Draw a line to match the rhyming pictures.

First . . . Next . . . Last

 Look at the pictures. Put them in the right order.

What comes <u>first</u>? Put a <u>1</u> in the box ☐ .

What comes <u>next</u>? Put a <u>2</u> in the box ☐ .

What comes <u>last</u>? Put a <u>3</u> in the box ☐ .

<u>Skill</u>: sequencing events to complete a picture story

First . . . Next . . . Last

 Look at the pictures. Put them in the right order.

What comes <u>first</u>? Put a <u>1</u> in the box ⬜ .

What comes <u>next</u>? Put a <u>2</u> in the box ⬜ .

What comes <u>last</u>? Put a <u>3</u> in the box ⬜ .

<u>Skill</u>: sequencing events to complete a picture story

Opposites

over

under

   1. Color the going <u>over</u> blue.

2. Color the going <u>under</u> green.

noisy

quiet

   1. Color the <u>noisy</u> yellow.

2. Color the <u>quiet</u> red.

<u>Skill</u>: understanding opposite relationships; following directions

More/Less

 Draw a circle around the box that has <u>more</u>.

1.

2.

 Draw a circle around the box that has <u>less</u>.

3.

4.

<u>Skill</u>: understanding concepts of <u>more</u> and <u>less</u>

163

I can read!

Read each sentence. Draw a circle around **yes** or **no.**

1. Can a [car] go?

   yes   **no**

2. Can a [balloon] pop?

   yes   **no**

3. Is an [ice cream cone] hot?

   yes   **no**

4. Can a [fish] run?

   yes   **no**

Skill: using picture clues to read and answer questions

Paths

Trace the paths. Start at the top.

More Paths

Follow the best path.

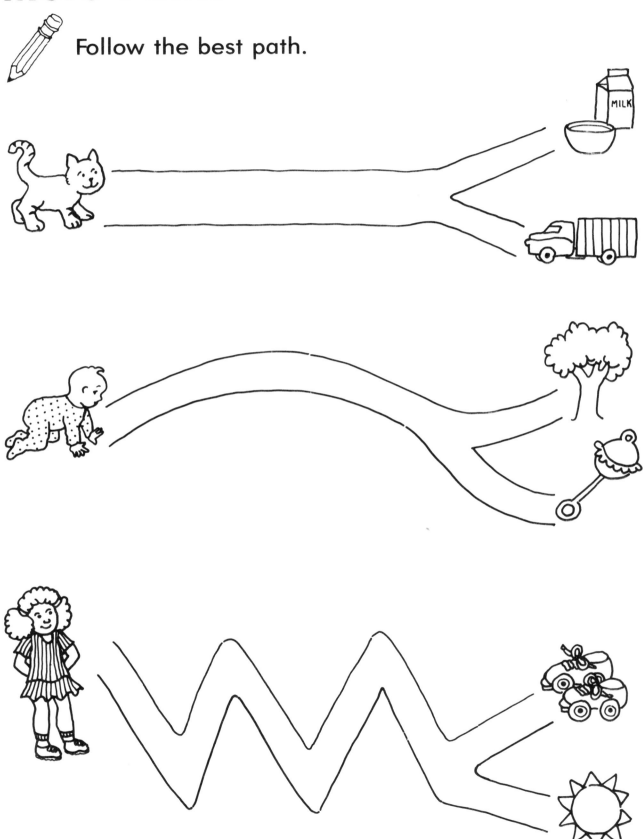

Skill: using eye-hand coordination to trace left-to-right paths

Maze Fun

 Draw a line from the to the .

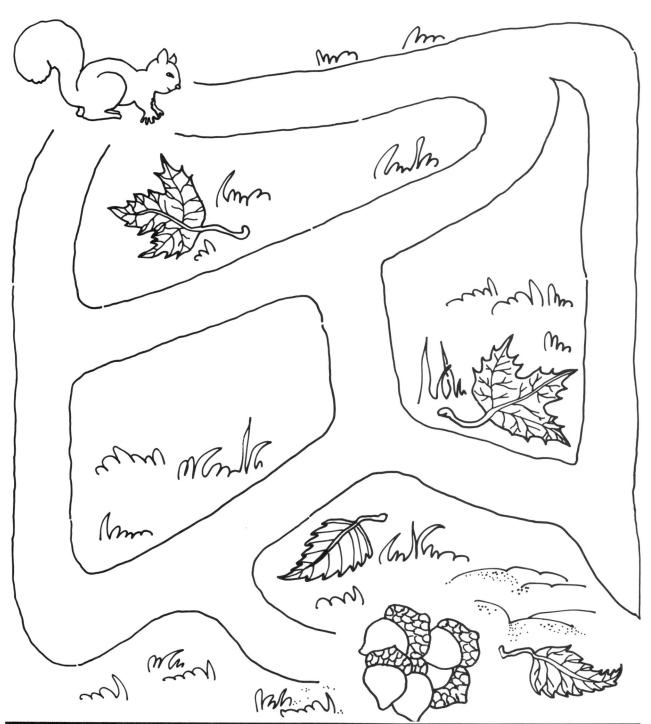

Match the Shapes

 Draw a line from each shape to its matching shape.

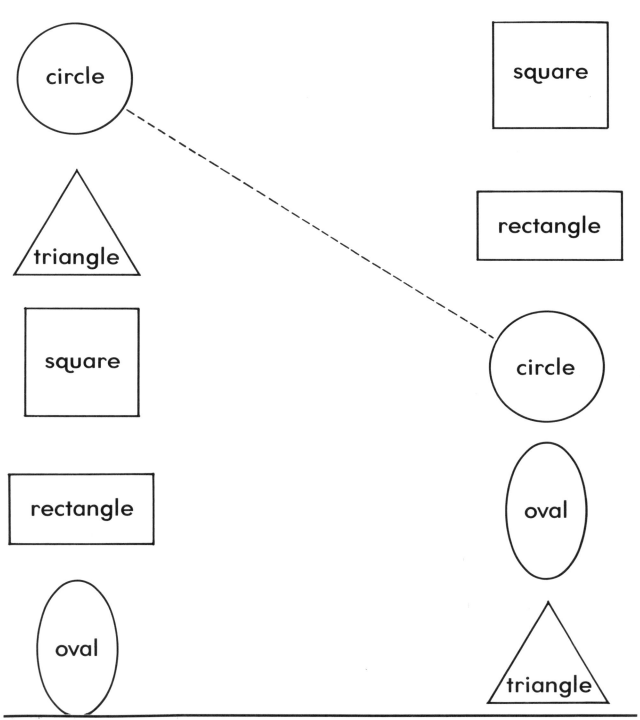

<u>Skill</u>: finding the matching shapes

Hidden Shapes

Color the shapes hidden in the picture.

▭ = red
□ = blue
○ = green
△ = yellow

Skill: identifying and locating geometric shapes

169

More and Less

more   less

 Draw a circle around the one in each row that has **more.**

 Draw a circle around the one in each row that has **less.**

 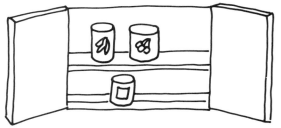

<u>Skill</u>: understanding the concepts of <u>more</u> and <u>less</u>

Short—Long

short   **long**

Circle the one that is **short.**

Circle the one that is **long.**

Dot to Dot

Start with the letter <u>A</u>. Draw a line to connect the dots in order A to Z.

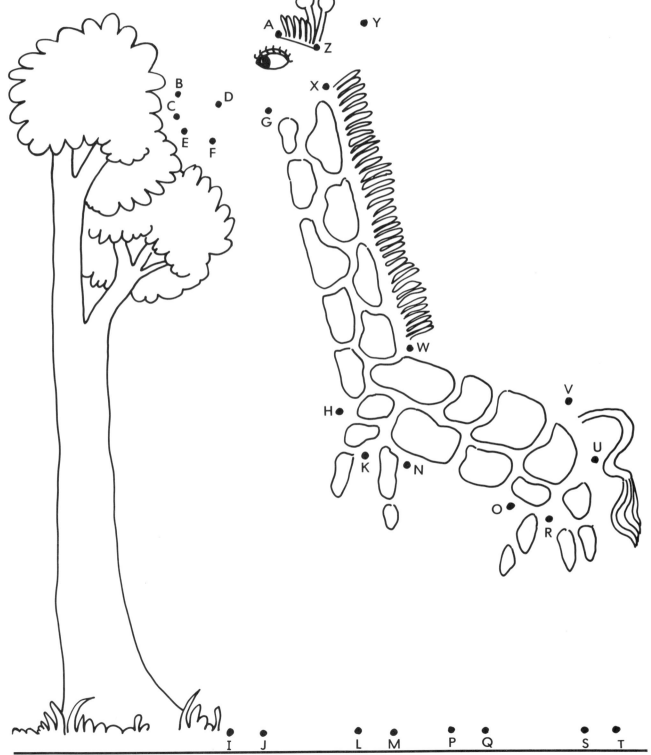

<u>Skill</u>: sequencing the letters A-Z in alphabetical order

Small—Big

small

big

Color the one that is **big.**

Color the one that is **small.**

Skill: using visual perception to make size comparisons

173

Smallest—Biggest

Color the **smallest.**

Color the **biggest.**

Skill: using visual perception to make size comparisons

Same

 Look at the pictures in each row. Draw a circle around the picture that is the **same** as the picture in the box.

Skill: using visual discrimination to match pictures   175

GETTING READY FOR READING & MATH

Same

 Look at the pictures in each box.
Circle **yes** if they are the same.
Circle **no** if they are not the same.

yes no

yes no

yes no

yes no

Skill: recognizing matching pictures and the words yes and no

Different

Look at the pictures in each row.
Put an X on the one that is **different.**

<u>Skill</u>: using visual discrimination to identify the picture that is different

Missing Parts

Look at the picture.
Draw **4** things that are missing.
Color the picture.

<u>Skill</u>: recognizing missing parts in a picture

Rhyming Pictures

 Say the name of each picture. Draw a circle around the picture in each row that rhymes with the picture in the box.

boat	star	goat	frog
clock	sock	cat	bell
tree	mouse	fan	bee
top	dog	mop	ball
pig	wig	duck	house

Skill: matching pictures of rhyming words

179

Patterns

 Look at the patterns. Circle the picture that comes next.

Opposites

Look at each picture. Find its opposite
at the bottom of the page.

happy

in

empty

dirty

 Cut out the pictures below. Paste each one
next to its opposite.

sad

out

full

clean

Skill: understanding opposite relationships

181

What's Wrong in the Picture?

Look at the picture.
Circle 7 things that are wrong.

Skill: using visual discrimination to identify what does not belong

One for Each

Draw a line from each animal to one food.

How Many?

 Count the pictures in each box.
Draw a circle around the right number.

1   2   3   4   5

<u>Skill</u>: matching the number of members in a set to the correct numeral

GETTING READY FOR READING & MATH

 Draw a line from each number to the set with the same number of objects.

 Color the pictures.

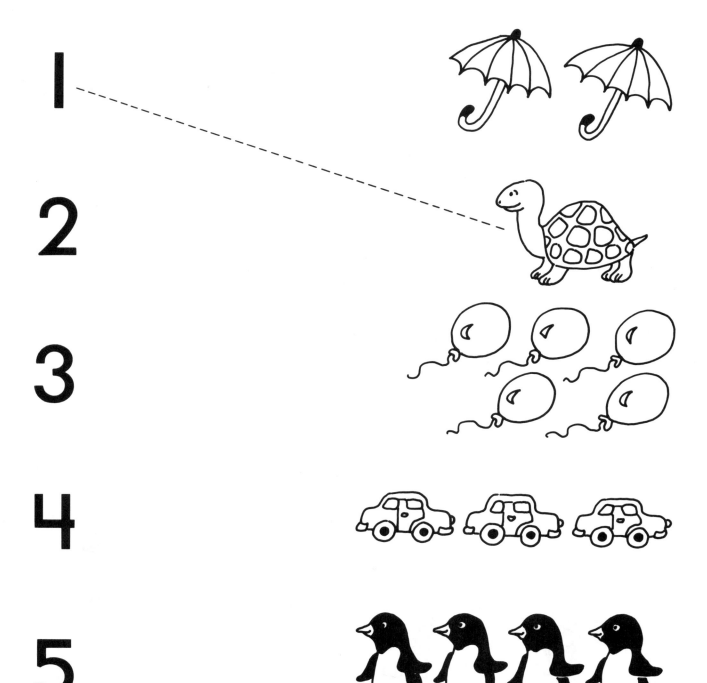

1

2

3

4

5

Matching Sets

Count the pictures in each row.

Draw a circle around the right number.

<u>Skill</u>: matching the number of members in a set to the correct numeral

First—Last

 Circle the one who is **first**.

Draw a line under the one who is **last**.

Skill: recognizing first and last

First. . .Next. . .Last

Look at the pictures.
What happens <u>first</u>? Put a <u>1</u> in the box ☐.
What happens <u>next</u>? Put a <u>2</u> in the box ☐.
What happens <u>last</u>? Put a <u>3</u> in the box ☐.

188

<u>Skill</u>: sequencing events to tell a story

What Comes Next?

 Look at the pictures in each row. Color the small picture that shows what you think will happen next.

Skill: identifying logical consequences

189

Story Order

Look at the pictures. Write the missing numbers in order. Draw an ending for the story. Color all the pictures.

Skill: inferring the outcome of a story sequence

Beginning Sounds

 Look at the picture in the box. Say its name. Color the pictures in each row that begin with the same sound.

 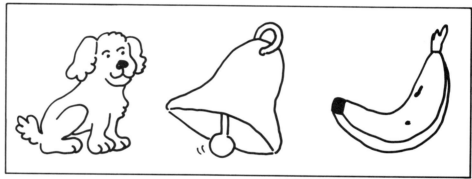

Skill: matching pictures with the same beginning sound

191

Beginning Sounds

 Draw a line from each picture to another picture that begins with the same sound.

Skill: matching pictures with the same beginning sound

What Belongs?

 Look at the pictures. Color the pictures in each row that belong together.

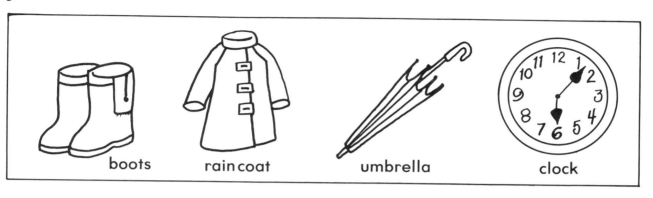

boots   raincoat   umbrella   clock

penny   cake   dime   quarter

duck   chicken   sun   turkey

elephant   banana   apple   grapes

<u>Skill</u>: classifying objects into logical categories

Summer or Winter?

boat

mittens

skates

summer

winter

sled

raft

pail

 Draw a line from each object to the picture where it belongs.

Skill: classifying objects according to seasons

What Doesn't Belong?

 Look at the picture. Color the five things that do not belong.

Skill: using visual discrimination to identify what doesn't belong; counting   195

Opposites

 Find the pictures that are opposites. Draw a line.

hot

out

big

cold

over

little

in

under

Skill: matching opposites

More Opposites

 Find the pictures that are opposites. Draw a line.

up

right

left

short

long

down

What Belongs Together?

 Look at the first two pictures in each row. Think of how they go together. Look at the next picture. Cut and paste the picture that goes with it.

dog   doghouse

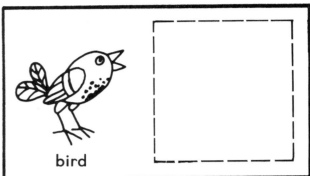

bird

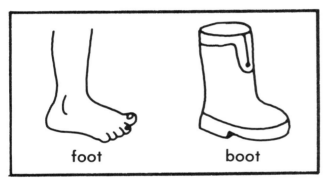

foot   boot

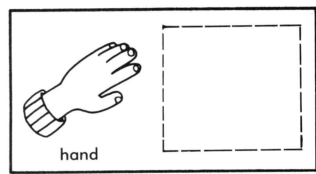

hand

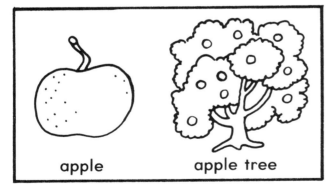

apple   apple tree

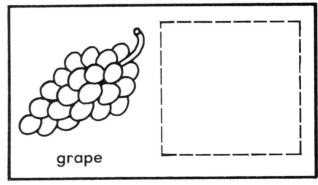

grape

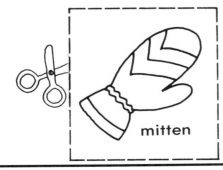

mitten

nest

grapevine

Skill: understanding specific relationships between objects

Beginning Sounds

 Look at the picture in each box. Say its name. Color the pictures in each row that **begin** with the same sound.

Skill: recognizing beginning sounds

199

More Beginning Sounds

 Look at the pictures. Say their names.
Draw a line to match the pictures that begin with
the same sound.

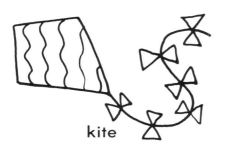

kite

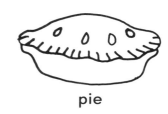

pie

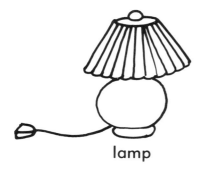

lamp

key

pig

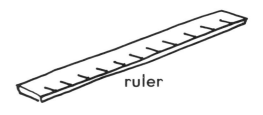

ruler

ring

lion

Skill: matching pictures with the same beginning sound

Beginning Letters

Look at the pictures of the toys. Say their names.

  Trace the letters. Write them.

doll

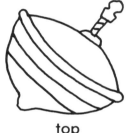

 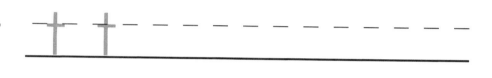

top

 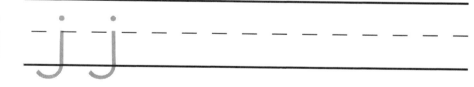

jacks

 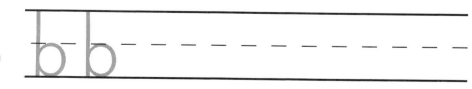

ball

Find the Beginning Letters

Color the spaces with **d** words red.
Color the spaces with **b** words blue.
Color the spaces with **m** words yellow.
Color the spaces with **n** words green.

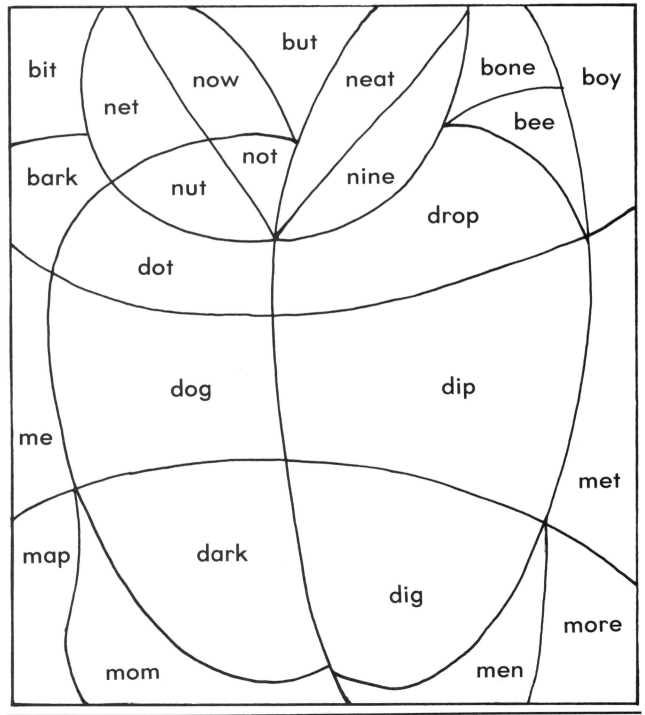

<u>Skill</u>: discriminating beginning letters; completing a picture by using a color code

More Beginning Letters

 Say the name of each picture.
Trace the beginning letter.

 six

 nut

 house

 Say the name of each picture.
Write the beginning letter.

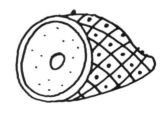

 aw

 ine

 am

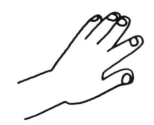

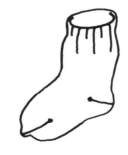

 and

 ock

et

Skill: writing beginning letters; making sound/symbol associations

203

Rhyming Words

 Look at the pictures. Say their names. Draw a line to match the rhyming pictures.

More Rhymes

 Pat likes things that rhyme with her name.
Draw a line to match her with each thing she likes.
Color the pictures.

bug

hat

bat

cat

Pat

crab

witch

Words with a

 Say the name of each picture. Write the letter **a** to finish each word.

s a d   c _ p   c _ n

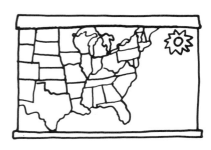

m _ n   b _ t   m _ p

r _ t   j _ m   p _ n

Skill: recognizing and writing short **a** words

Words with e

Hen and pen have the same middle sound.

Say the name of each picture. Draw lines from the hen to the pictures with the same middle sound.

hen

Write the letter **e** to finish each word.
Then say the word.

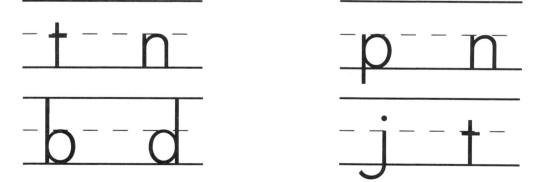

t __ n   p __ n

b __ d   j __ t

Skill: recognizing, writing and reading short **e** words

Words with i

 Write the letter **i** to finish each word. Draw a line to match each word with its picture.

s_i_x

p_g

b_b

f_sh

w_g

Skill: writing and reading short **i** words

Words with o

T<u>o</u>m and t<u>o</u>p have the same middle sound.

 Say the name of each picture. Draw lines from
T<u>o</u>m to the pictures with the same middle sound.

Tom

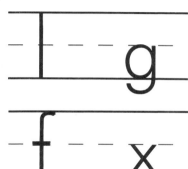

 Write the letter **o** to finish each word.
Then say the word.

l___g   m___p

f___x   fr___g

Words with u

Write the letter **u** to finish each word.

r u g

c _ p

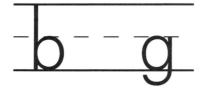

b _ g

n _ t

Find the pictures of the 4 words you just wrote. Color them.

<u>Skill</u>: writing and reading short **u** words

Which Letter?

 Trace the letters.

a   e   i   o   u

 Say the name of each picture. Write the correct letter to finish each word.

 h a t   t _ p   p _ n

 b _ s   c _ t   sh _ p

Skill: determining which letters are missing and writing them to make words

211

Ending Sounds

These 2 words have the same **ending** sound.

dog    pig

 Look at the picture in each box. Say its name. Color the pictures in each row that **end** with the same sound.

   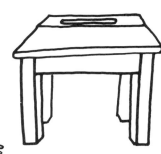

Skill: recognizing ending sounds

READING READINESS
Ending Sounds and Letters

Say the name of each picture. Listen to the ending sound

 Trace each ending letter.

elf

leaf

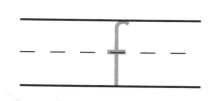
f

star

bear

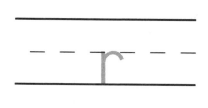
r

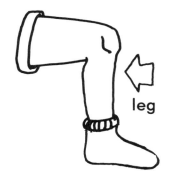

leg

dog

g

gum

broom

m

Skill: recognizing ending sounds and writing ending letters

Red and Yellow

 Trace each word. Write it on the line.

red

yellow

 Find the pictures that may be red. Color them red. Find the pictures that may be yellow. Color them yellow.

<u>Skill</u>: writing and reading color words; relating color to objects

Blue and Green

Trace each word. Write it on the line.

blue

green

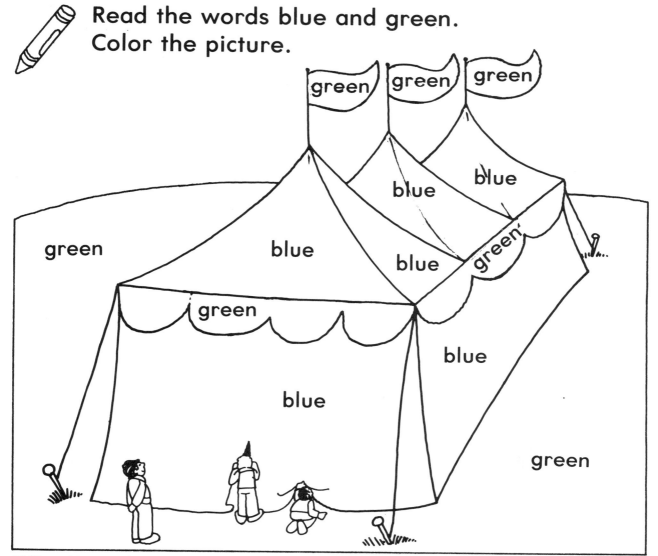

Read the words blue and green.
Color the picture.

green   green   green

blue   blue

green   blue   blue   green

green

green

blue   blue

blue

green

What Comes After?

 Look at the large pictures in each row. Draw a circle around the small picture that shows what comes **after** the other pictures.

216

<u>Skill</u>: using context to determine what comes **after**

Red, Yellow, Blue, Green

 Read the words red, yellow, blue, green.
Color the picture.

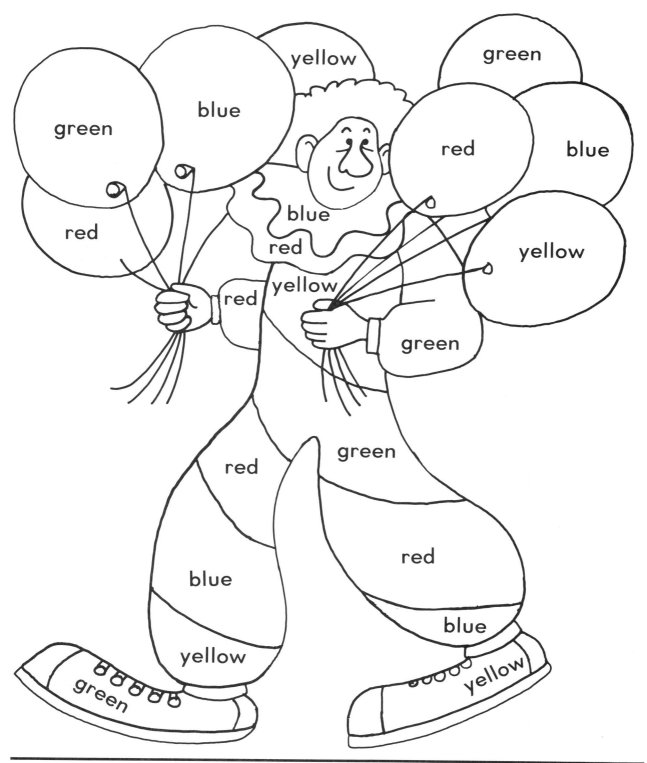

What Comes Before?

 Look at the pictures in the boxes. Draw a circle around the small picture that shows what came **before** the pictures in the boxes.

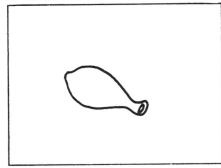

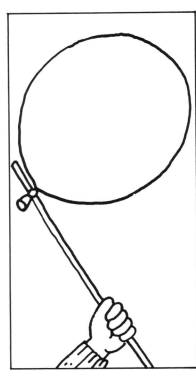

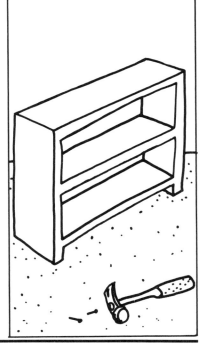

<u>Skill</u>: using context to determine what comes **before**

Story Order

 Look at the pictures. Four of them tell a story. Color the pictures that tell the story. Write numbers in the boxes to put the story in order.

Skill: recognizing parts of the same story; sequencing a story

219

Story Sense

 Look at the large pictures in each row. Color the small picture that shows what is more likely to happen next.

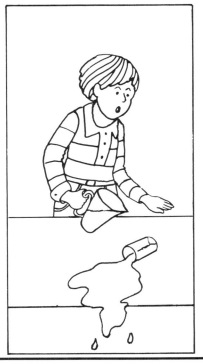

Skill: identifying logical consequences

What Is More Likely?

 Look at the large pictures in each row. Color the small picture that shows what is more likely to happen next.

Kim's Story

Look at the pictures of Kim.
They are in order to show how she grows older.

 Write the missing numbers in the boxes.

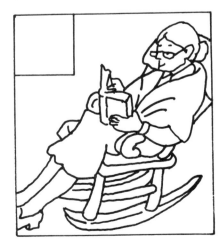

Skill: identifying chronological sequence; writing numbers in order

Sam's Story

Look at the pictures of Sam.
They are in order to show how he grows older.

Write the missing numbers in the boxes.

My Story

My name is _____.

My birthday is _____.

I am _____ years old.

I am ready to read!

Skill: reading and writing familiar information

Longer or Shorter?

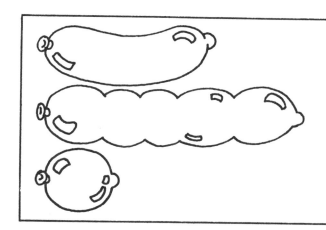

Nan's balloon

longer than Nan's balloon

shorter than Nan's balloon

 Use your blue crayon.
Color each  that is **longer** than Nan's.
Use your red crayon.
Color each that is **shorter** than Nan's.

Nan's

<u>Skill</u>: comparing objects using longer and shorter   225

Before or After?

| before | after |

 Look at the pictures. Color the picture in each row that shows which would happen **before** the other.

226   Skill: distinguishing between before and after

Between

This car is **between** two cars.

This horse is **between** two horses.

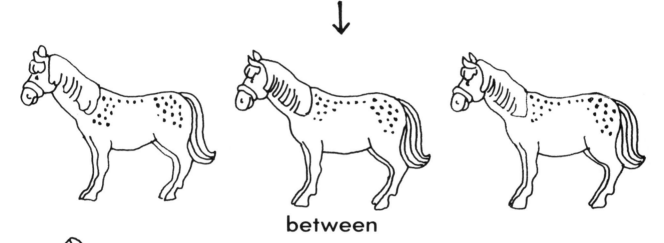

between

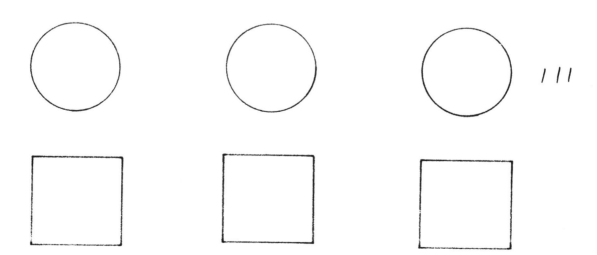

Color each shape that is **between** the others.

Hot or Cold?

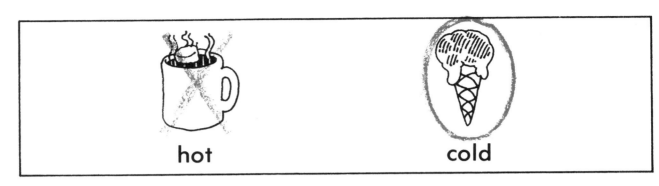

hot   cold

 Draw an X on each thing that is **hot.**
Draw a circle around each thing that is **cold.**

       Skill: indicating whether objects/scenes are hot or cold

MATH READINESS
Heavy or Light?

This is **heavy.**   This is **light.**

 Draw a circle around the object that is **heavier.**

 Draw a line under the object that is **lighter.**

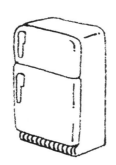   

Above or Below?

Complete page 229 before doing this page.

above

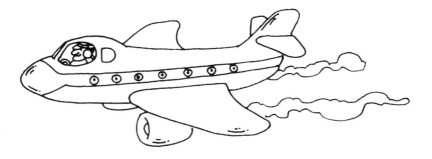

below

 Cut and paste these pictures **above** the plane.

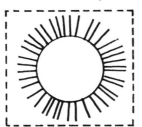

 Cut and paste these pictures **below** the plane.

Skill: placing objects above and below a given object

One for Each

There is one hat for each person. Draw a line to match each person to the right hat.

One and Two

I duck is colored.

 Color I duck.

 Trace the number. Write it on the line **one** time.

2 turtles are colored.

 Color 2 turtles.

 Trace the number. Write it on the lines **two** times.

232   <u>Skill</u>: understanding the meaning of the numbers one and two; writing 1 and 2

Three and Four

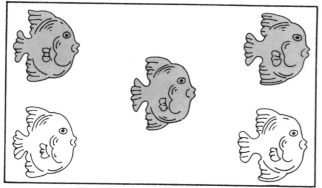 

3 fish are colored.   Color 3 fish.

 Trace the number. Write it on the lines **three** times.

4 rabbits are colored.   Color 4 rabbits.

 Trace the number. Write it on the lines **four** times.

Five

5 birds are colored.

 Color 5 birds.

Trace the number. Write it on the lines **five** times.

Skill: understanding the meaning of the number five; writing 5

Numbers in Order

 Look at each number. Count the 's.
Color the right number of 's in each row.

1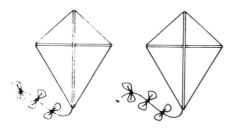

2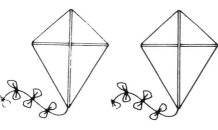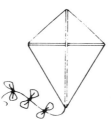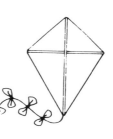

3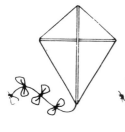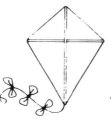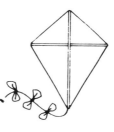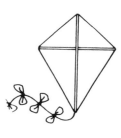

4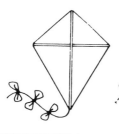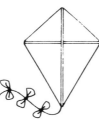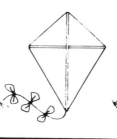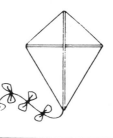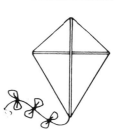

5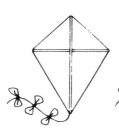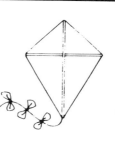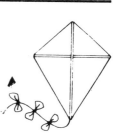

Same

This fishbowl has the **same** number of fish.

 Draw balloons so Holly will have the **same** number as Todd.

<u>Skill</u>: identifying and drawing sets with the same number

More and Less

more	less

 Color the set in each row that has **more.**

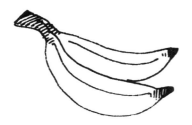

 Color the set in each row that has **less.**

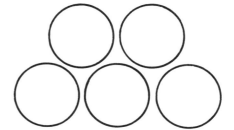

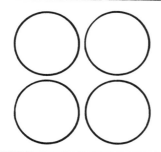

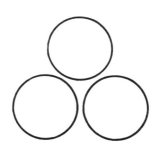

Problem Solving

 Look at the picture. Read the questions.
Draw a circle around the right number in
each row.

Count the 📻's. How many 📻's in all?	1	2	3
Count the ⚽'s. How many ⚽'s in all?	2	3	4
Count the ☕'s. How many ☕'s in all?	2	3	4

<u>Skill</u>: sorting to interpret pictures; counting

Using Pictures

 Look at each picture. Read the questions.
Draw a circle around the right number in
each row.

Count the 🐦's.

How many 🐦's in all?   1   2   3

Count the 📚's.

How many 📚's in all?   1   2   4

Count the 🐰's.

How many 🐰's in all?   1   3   5

Skill: sorting to interpret pictures; counting

Find the Leader

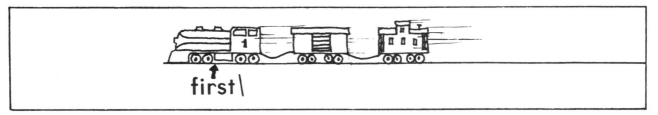

first

Draw a circle around the **first** one in each row.

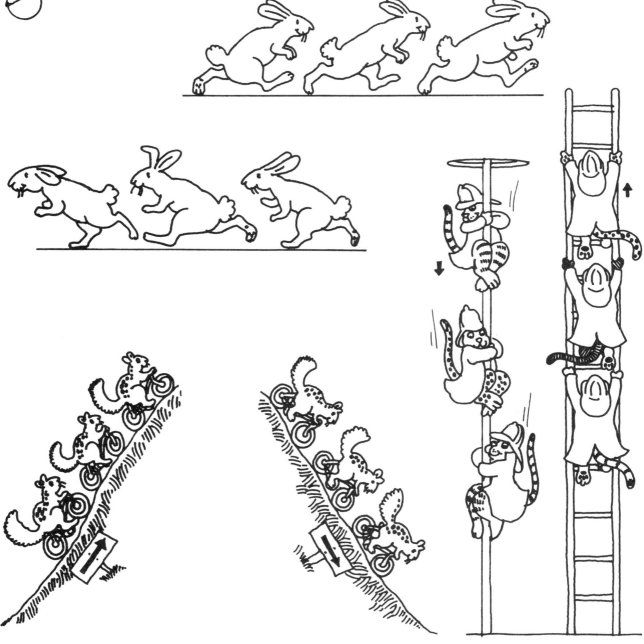

<u>Skill</u>: identifying the first object in a row

Square

Square ☐
All squares have 4 corners.
All 4 sides are the same length.
Squares may be different sizes.

Follow the path that has only ☐'s.

Color the ☐'s to help Sally get home.

Sally

Start

End

Skill: understanding the concept of square; identifying squares

Circle

Circle

Circles may be different sizes.

Here are more circles.

Color the one that is the biggest

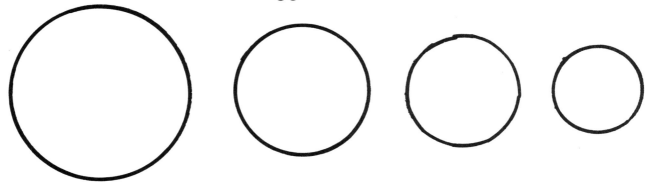

 We see many circles every day. Trace the circles to finish the picture.

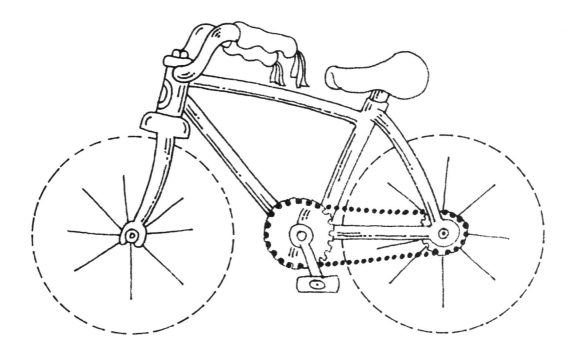

Skill: understanding the concept of circle; drawing circles

Triangle

Triangle △
All triangles have 3 sides.
Triangles may be different sizes. △ △ △

Trace the triangle shapes to finish this picture.

Color the picture.

Skill: understanding the concept of triangle; matching triangles to real objects with the same shape

243

Rectangle

Rectangle

All rectangles have 4 corners like squares.
Rectangles may be different sizes.

 Look at the shapes. Find the rectangles.
Color them.

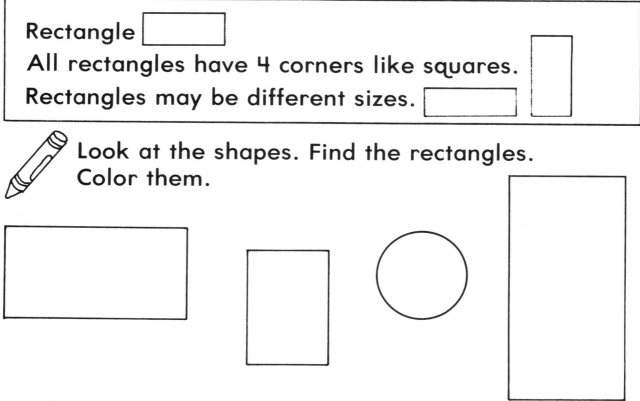

We see rectangles every day. Draw a circle around
each picture that has the shape of a rectangle.

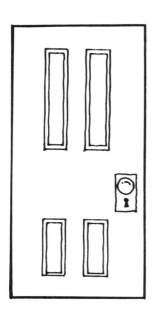

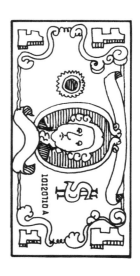

<u>Skill</u>: understanding the concept of rectangle; identifying rectangles

Shapes

Trace the shapes to finish this picture.
These are the shapes you will need to trace.

square   circle   triangle   rectangle

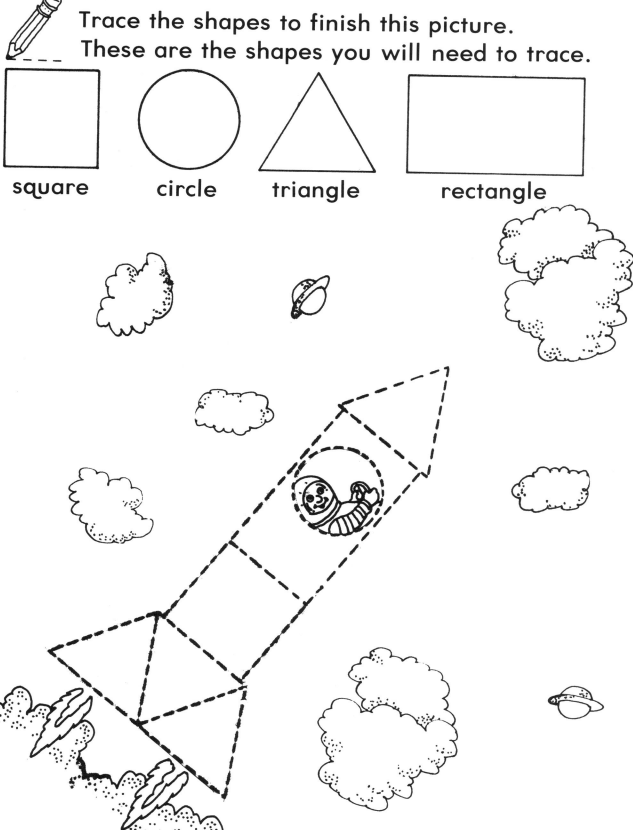

Skill: tracing squares, circles, triangles, rectangles

Matching Patterns

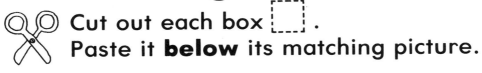 Cut out each box ⬜ .
Paste it **below** its matching picture.

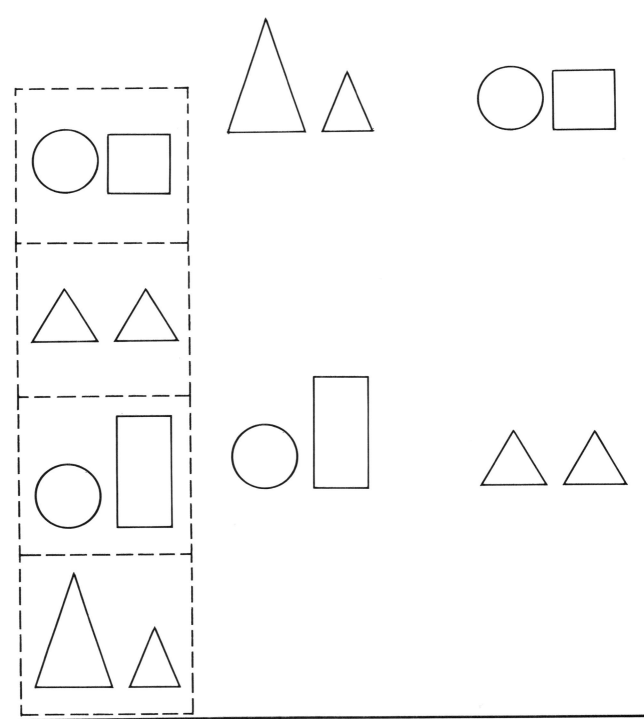

<u>Skill</u>: matching patterns; understanding the concept of below

More Patterns

 Color the shape that would come next in each row.

Color, Size, Shape

Look at all the shapes in the box.

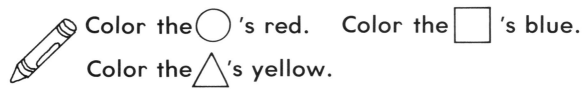

Color the ◯ 's red.   Color the ▢ 's blue.

Color the △ 's yellow.

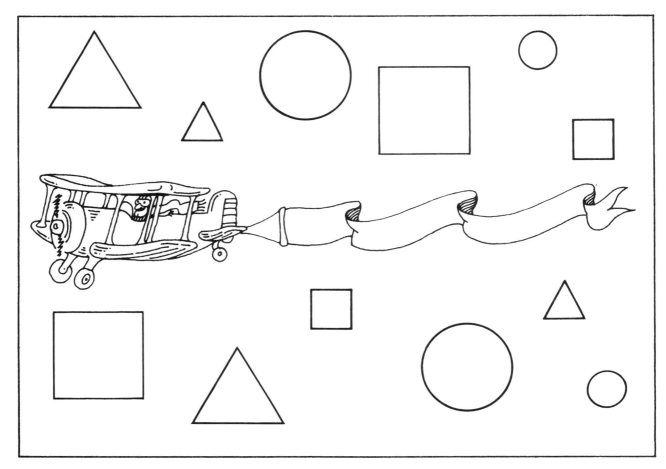

 Draw a line under the small red ◯ above
the ✈ .

Put an X on the large blue ▢ below
the ✈ .

Draw a circle around the small yellow △
above the ✈ .

Skill: classifying shapes; following directions

One Half

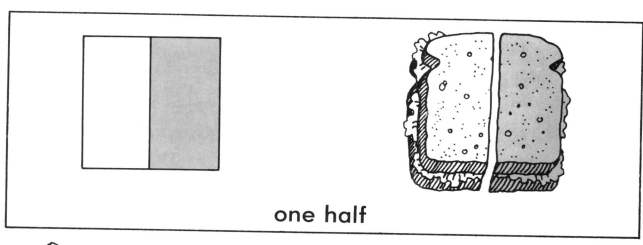

one half

 Draw a line under each picture that shows **one half** colored in.

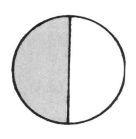 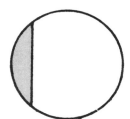 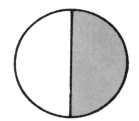

  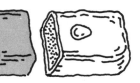

 Draw a line to divide each picture in **half.**

Skill: recognizing, then determining one half

Zero

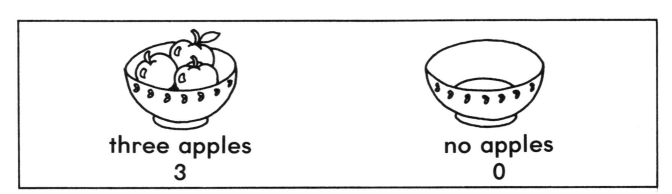

three apples
3

no apples
0

 Which ones are empty? Draw a circle around the ones with no objects inside.

 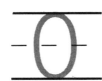

<u>Skill</u>: identifying groups with no objects; associating 0 with sets with no objects

What Time Is It?

What time is it? Draw hands on the clock to show the time right now. Trace the numbers.

Skill: recognizing a clock face and associating clocks with time

251

Time of Day

Look at the pictures in each row. Draw a circle around the picture that shows what happens first.

8:00　　　　morning　　　　**7:30**

12:00　　　　noon　　　　**12:30**

9:00　　　　night　　　　**6:30**

Note to Parent: Notice the time shown below each picture. Talk about the time you do these things in your own family.

Skill: associating time of day with order of events

How Much Time?

Look at each row.
Color the picture that takes **more** time.

<u>Skill</u>: indicating which activity takes more time

253

Penny, Nickel, Dime

Look at the three different coins.

penny   nickel   dime

   Color each penny brown.
Draw a circle around each nickel.
Draw a line under each dime.

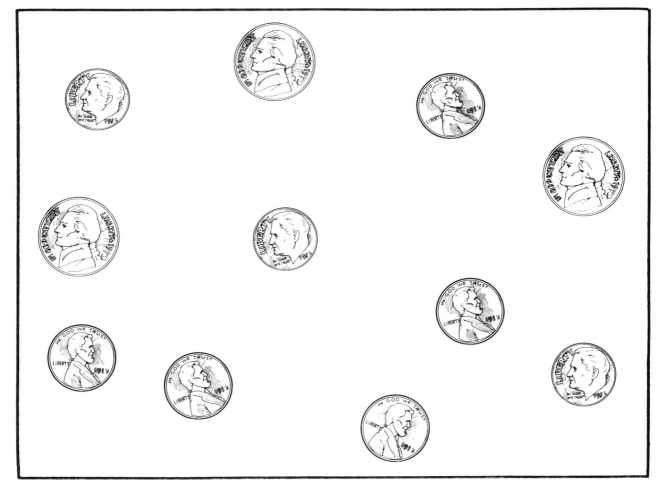

<u>Skill</u>: identifying penny, nickel, and dime

Matching Money

 Draw a line to match the amounts of money that are the same.

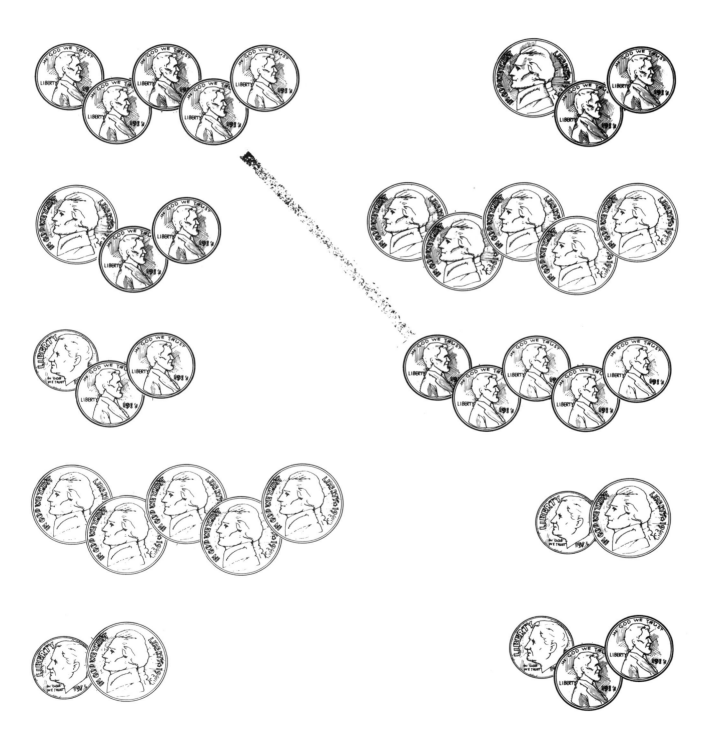

Skill: discriminating among penny, nickel and dime; matching same sets

255

Certificate

name: _____

has done super work!

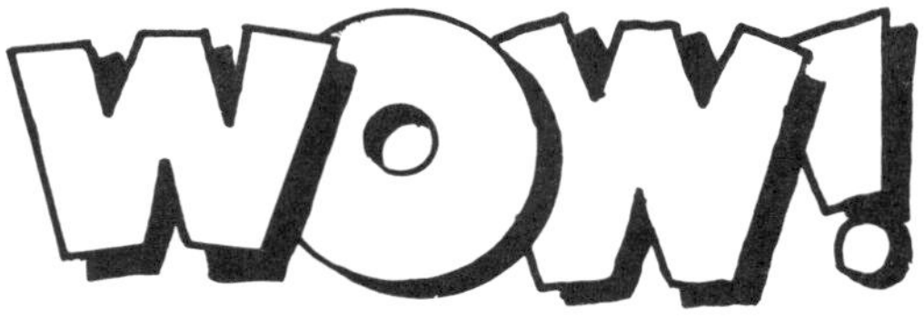

Great Job

WOW!

MY FIRST WORDS

See it. Say it. Write it. Read it.

The   the

The [boy]

The [girl]

1-2-3-4-5

I see the

[boy]   [girl]

MY FIRST WORDS

See it. Say it. Write it. Read it.

See   see

See   see

I see a  .

boy

I see a .

frog

The will go.

frog

258

Skill: vocabulary development—See, see

MY FIRST WORDS

✏️ See it. Say it. Write it. Read it.

go   **go**   **go**

go   *go*

See the frog go!
Follow the path with go.

go

see   is   see

go   the

the   go   the   see

is   is   the

go

see   go   go

is   go

the

Skill: vocabulary review—see, go

MY FIRST WORDS

✏️ See it. Say it. Write it. Read it.

in

in

out

out

🖍️ Write the word. Color the pictures.

The 🦭 is _____
seal   _____.

The 🦭 is _____
seal   _____.

Skill: vocabulary development—in, out

MY FIRST WORDS

Circle Yes or No

The dog is in.　　Yes　　No

The cat is in.　　Yes　　No

The dog is out.　　Yes　　No

The cat is out.　　Yes　　No

MY FIRST WORDS

Color Words

See it. Say it. Write it. Read it.
Color the pictures.

red

blue

green

yellow

An ___ apple ___ is _____ .

A ___ tree ___ is _____ .

A ___ chick ___ is _____ .

A ___ lake ___ is _____ .

Skill: Skill: vocabulary development—color words

MY FIRST WORDS
Color Puzzle

Read the word. Color the spaces.

. red   .. blue

∴ green   ∴ yellow

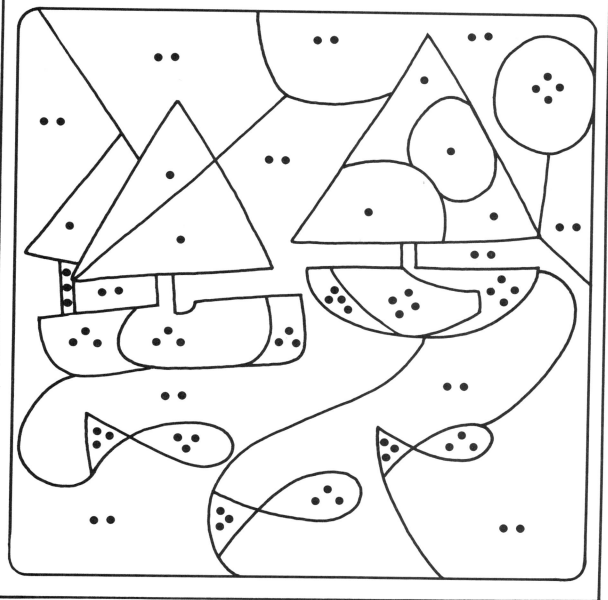

MY FIRST WORDS

See it. Say it. Write it. Read it.

big

big

little

little

A 🐦 is _____ .

bird

An 🐘 is _____ .

elephant

◆ Circle the correct word. Write it.

A 🐭 is _____ .

mouse

big   little

A 🦛 is _____ .

hippo

big   little

Skill: vocabulary development—big, little

MY FIRST WORDS

Read the sentences. Color the pictures.

Color the big 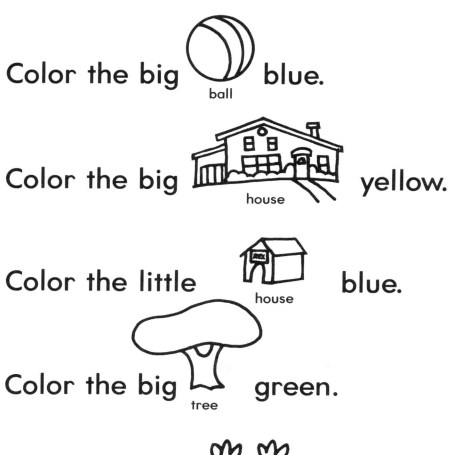 blue.
ball

Color the big [house] yellow.
house

Color the little [house] blue.
house

Color the big [tree] green.
tree

Color the little [flowers] red.
flowers

MY FIRST WORDS

run

run

jump

jump

Read the sentences. Circle Yes or No.

A turtle can run.   Yes   No

A kangaroo can jump.   Yes   No

A girl can run.   Yes   No

A tree can jump.   Yes   No

A boy can jump.   Yes   No

Skill: vocabulary development—run, jump

The Race

Read the story.

1, 2, 3 go!

Run run!
bear

Go dog go!

Jump, jump, jump!

MY FIRST WORDS

See it. Say it. Write it. Read it.

Draw a line to match the word to its shape. Write the word in its shape.

pink

pink

black

black

brown

brown

pink

Color the pictures.

black   pink   brown

Skill: vocabulary development—black, brown, pink

MY FIRST WORDS

✏️ Read the sentences. Color the picture.

Color the big 🐻 black.
bear

Color the little 🚂 red.
train

Color the big 🌲 green.
tree

Color the little 🦩 pink.
flamingo

Color the little 🐴 brown.
pony

Color the big 〰️ blue.
pond

Color the little 🦆🦆 yellow.
ducks

See it. Say it. Write it. Read it.

Can

can

Can

can

The  girl can.

The boy can.

Can the dog ?

MY FIRST WORDS

 Look at the words.
Draw a circle around the word in each row that
is the same as the word in the box.

can	and out can
blue	black blue see
run	run can big
jump	little jump go
The	Blue Out The

Picture Dictionary

Read the sentences. Draw a line from each little picture to the word that tells about it.

1. See the _____ .   • boy

2. I can see the _____ .   • woman

3. I can see a _____ .   • girl

4. See the little _____ .   • train

Skill: using picture clues to develop vocabulary

MY FIRST WORDS

See it. Say it. Write it. Read it.

like

_____

_ _ _ _ _ _ _ _ _

_____

likes

_____

_ _ _ _ _ _ _ _ _

_____

Read the sentences. Draw a circle around the correct word. Write it in the blank.

1. I _____
       like   likes   bananas.

2. The girl _____
       like   likes   grapes.

3. I _____
       like   likes   popcorn.

4. The _____
       lion   like   likes   meat.

5. The _____
       giraffes   like   likes   leaves.

MY FIRST WORDS

See it. Say it. Write it. Read it.

not

not

fast

fast

Read the sentences. Circle Yes or No.

1. A turtle can run fast.   Yes   No

2. A bus can not sing.   Yes   No

3. A train can not go fast.   Yes   No

4. The sun is not green.   Yes   No

5. A fish can swim fast.   Yes   No

6. An elephant is not little.   Yes   No

Skill: vocabulary development–not, fast

Riddles

Read each riddle. Draw a line to the right picture.

1.
I am green.
I can go fast.
I am a _____ .

2.
I am big.
I can go fast.
I am an _____ .

3.
I am big.
I am yellow.
I am a _____ .

4.
I am little.
I am orange.
I am a _____ .

5.
I can jump.
I am brown.
I am a _____ .

6.
I am fast.
I can run.
I am a _____ .

Skill: vocabulary development

MY FIRST WORDS

See it. Say it. Write it. Read it.

dig

dig

swim

swim

sing

sing

fly

fly

Draw a line to the word that completes each sentence.

1. A dog will _____ .

2. A kite can _____ .

3. A fish can _____ .

4. A girl can _____ .

- swim
- dig
- fly
- sing

276

Skill: vocabulary development

MY FIRST WORDS

See it. Say it. Write it. Read it.

We

will

Read the sentences. Draw a line to the correct picture.

We will run.

We will sing.

We will fly.

We will jump.

We will dig.

MY FIRST WORDS

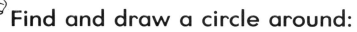
Find and draw a circle around:

Skill: developing visual discrimination

MY FIRST WORDS

🔖 Find the correct sentence. ✂️ Cut it out.
Paste it under the correct picture.

| The dog likes to dig. | This bird likes to sing. |
| Do you like to swim? | This can fly fast. |

Make a Book

◀ Follow the directions to make your own book.

1. Take the next page out of this book.

2. Cut on the dotted line.

3. Fold on the solid line.

4. Put the pages in order by number.

5. Staple on the folded edge.

The Zoo Train

MY FIRST WORDS

See it. Say it. Write it. Read it.

Play

play

Put an X in the box next to the sentence that tells about each picture.

☐ The dog will play.

☐ The dog will not play.

☐ The girl will play.

☐ The girl will not play.

☐ Do not play here.

☐ Play here.

MY FIRST WORDS

 Read the sentences. Follow the directions.

1. The [tent] is big. Color it green.

2. The [canoe] is on the [car].
   Color it orange.

3. This is a big [fire].
   Color it red.

4. The [squirrels] run fast.

   Color 2 brown.

Skill: following directions

MY FIRST WORDS

See it. Say it. Write it. Read it.

this

fun

Read the sentences.
Draw a line to the correct picture.

This is little.

This is black.

This is fun.

This is not fun.

Fun on the Slide

Follow the slide. Color all the boxes with the word <u>fun</u> in them.

<u>Skill</u>: vocabulary review

MY FIRST WORDS

See it. Say it. Write it. Read it.

do

you

Read the play.

Do you like to run?

Yes. I like to run.

Do you like to jump?

Yes. I like to jump.

Do you like to sing?

Yes. I like to sing.

Do you like to swim?

No! I do not like to swim.

<u>Skill</u>: vocabulary development—do, you

MY FIRST WORDS

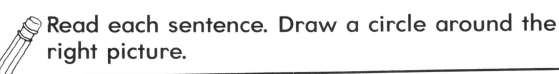 Read each sentence. Draw a circle around the right picture.

1. You can jump on it.

2. The woman will fly it.

3. This is fun!

4. You can play with this.

5. You can not do it.

<u>Skill</u>: understanding sentences

Hidden Pictures

Color the words that begin with b   blue.

Color the words that begin with s   green.

Color the words that begin with p   brown.

Color the words that begin with l   pink.

Color the words that begin with d   yellow.

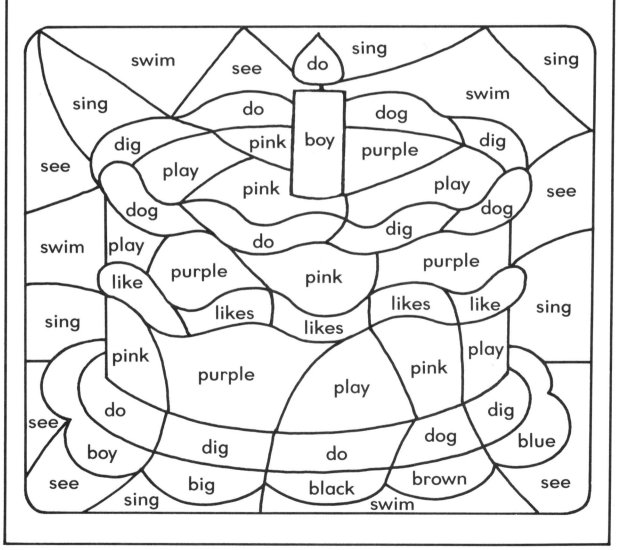

Skill: vocabulary review

MY FIRST WORDS

Read the words. Draw a picture.

black cat	a purple hat
a little green bird	A big brown dog

<u>Skill</u>: vocabulary review

See it. Say it. Write it. Read it.

Make   make

_____   _____

- - - - - - - - - -   - - - - - - - - - -

_____   _____

Read the sentences. Look at the picture. Write the number in the box.

1. We will make this. →

2. I will make this.   →

3. I will make this red. →

MY FIRST WORDS

Color the words the color that is named in the list below.

brown	**yellow**	**green**	**blue**
you	can	fly	this
jump		on	girl
play		it	little

Skill: vocabulary review

MY FIRST WORDS

See it. Say it. Write it. Read it.

Who

Whoooo?

Read the sentences. Find the correct picture.
Write the number in the box.

1. Who will make this?

2. Who will make this?

3. Who will make this?

This Is a Play

 Draw a circle around the correct answers.
Who is in this play?

boy   mouse   princess   horse

prince   lion   frog   giant

Skill: vocabulary development–play

MY FIRST WORDS

 See it. Say it. Write it. Read it.

with

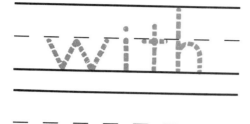

me

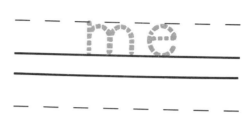

Read the sentences. Draw a line.

I will go on a train.

Will you go with me?

I will go on a  .
jet

Will you go with me?

I will go in a  .
car

Will you go with me?

MY FIRST WORDS

Read the sentence. Draw a picture of something you can play with.

You can play with this.

Draw a circle around the right word to finish each sentence. Write it on the line.

I can run with _____.

you   we

The woman will not dig with _____.

it   the

The boy can _____.

pink   play

The man will sing with _____.

fly   this

MY FIRST WORDS

dog man boy girl cat

1. Who will play with this?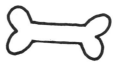

   _____

   A _____ will play with it.

2. Who will play with this?

   _____

   The _____ will play with it.

3. Who will play with this?

   _____   _____

   A _____ and a _____

   will play with it.

4. Who will play this?

   _____

   A _____ will play it.

Picture Dictionary

Write the correct word.

Skill: vocabulary development–truck, bus, car, jet

MY FIRST WORDS

Draw a line from the picture to the correct word.

Truck

Car

Bus

Train

Jet

Way to Go

| car | bus | truck | jet |

 Write a word to complete the sentence.

1. A _____ can fly fast.

2. A cat can not take a
_____
_____.

3. We can go to the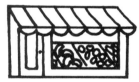
store
_____
in a _____.

4. A big _____
will do this.

Skill: vocabulary review—car, bus, truck, jet

Truck Stop

 Follow directions.

1. Color the big truck red.

2. Color the little car green.

3. Color the little truck blue.

4. Color the bus yellow.

5. Color the big car black.

6. Color the jet orange.

Crossword Puzzle

Write the words in the puzzle.

Down   Across

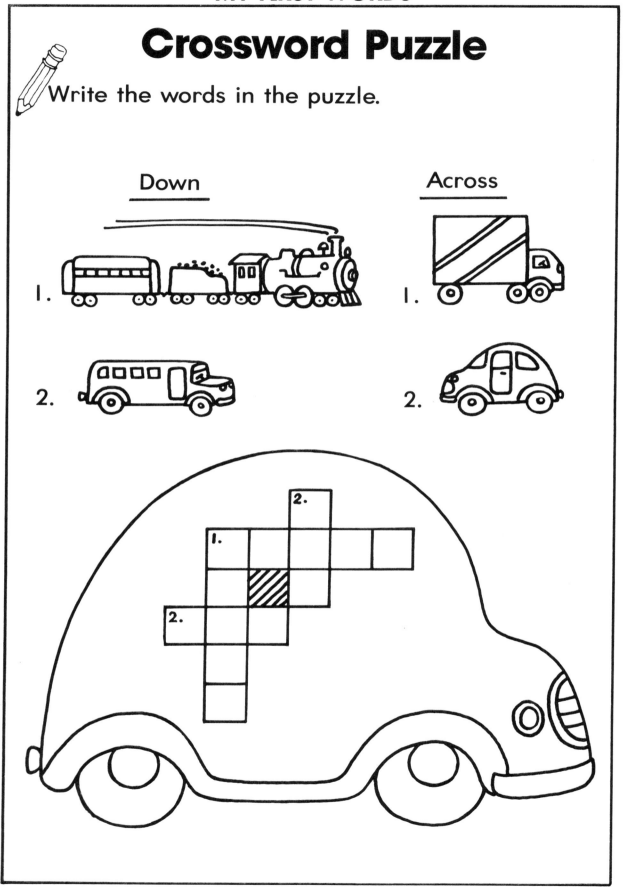

1.   1.

2.   2.

<u>Skill</u>: vocabulary review

MY FIRST WORDS

See it. Say it. Write it. Read it.

ride
_____
- - - - - - - - - - - -
_____

up

_____
- - - - - - - - - - - -
_____

down

_____
- - - - - - - - - - - -
_____

Read the sentences. Circle Yes or No.

1. The 🪁 kite is up.   Yes   No

2. The girl is down.   Yes   No

3. The boy can not ride.   Yes   No

MY FIRST WORDS

Read the story.

The roller coaster can go down.

The girl on the ferris wheel is up.

We can ride in the cable cars.

✏️ Write the correct word in the blank.

_____

The roller coaster can go _____.

_____

The girl on the ferris wheel is _____.

_____

We can _____ in the cable cars.

Skill: vocabulary review—up, down, ride

MY FIRST WORDS

✏️ See it. Say it. Write it. Read it.

are   ## happy

_____   _____

- - - - - - - - -   - - - - - - - - -

_____   _____

Read the sentences. Draw a line to the correct picture.

1. The ___ **are happy.**
   clowns

2. The ___ **are not happy.**
   clowns

3. The ___ **are happy.**
   babies

4. The ___ **are not happy.**
   babies

Skill: vocabulary development—are, happy   305

MY FIRST WORDS

See it. Say it. Write it. Read it.

school

_____

- - - - - - - - - - -

_____

store

_____

- - - - - - - - - - -

_____

house

_____

- - - - - - - - - - -

_____

school   store   house

Write one of these words to finish each sentence.

house   school   store

_____

We are in - - - - - - - - - - - -

_____ .

_____

We are in the - - - - - - - - -

_____ .

_____

We are in a - - - - - - - - - -

_____ .

Skill: vocabulary development—school, store, house

MY FIRST WORDS

Draw a line from the picture to the place you would find it.

Read the Story

We like this house.

We can play in it.

We have fun in it.

Do you like this house?

Skill: vocabulary review—house

MY FIRST WORDS

See it. Say it. Write it. Read it.

help

help

me

me

Read each story. Write help or me to finish the sentence.

"I will help you."

"No.
You are too little to _____."

"I will help you."

"Yes! You can
_____

help_____."

MY FIRST WORDS

Do you like to help?
Draw a picture to show how you help.

I can help Mother.

I can help a little boy.

Who will help? Draw a line to the right picture.

310

<u>Skill</u>: vocabulary review

Number Words

one
1

two
2

three
3

four
4

five
5

 Color the correct number of objects.

Color three.

Color one.

Color five.

Color two.

Color four.

Skill: vocabulary development—one, two, three, four, five

311

MY FIRST WORDS

✏️ Look at the picture.
Read the sentence. Circle Yes or No.

1. I can see three 🐰🐰 .   Yes   No
rabbits

2. I can see two 🦌 .   Yes   No
deer

3. I can see five 🐿️🐿️ .   Yes   No
squirrels

4. I can see four 🦨🦨 .   Yes   No
skunks

5. I can see five 🐦🐦 .   Yes   No
birds

Skill: vocabulary review—number words

MY FIRST WORDS

Follow directions.

1. Draw two yellow flowers .

2. Draw four green balls .

3. Draw five brown boxes .

4. Draw one red car .

See it. Say it. Write it. Read it.

Where

did

Where did it go?

Look at the first picture. Look at the second picture. What is missing? Where did it go? Draw an X on the correct place.

Where is it?

Where is it?

Skill: vocabulary development—where, did

MY FIRST WORDS

 See it. Say it. Write it. Read it.

They

they

Read the sentences.
Draw a line to the correct picture.

1. They are in school.

2. They are little.

3. They are happy.

4. They are up.

Skill: vocabulary development—they

315

Where Did They Go?

Look at the pictures.
Read the sentences.
Draw a line to the correct picture.

1.

Where did they go?

2.

Where did they go?

3.

Where did they go?

4.

Where did they go?

Skill: vocabulary review—where, did, they

Puzzle Page

Read the words in the box.
Read the clues.
Write the words in the correct places.

blue red purple pink black

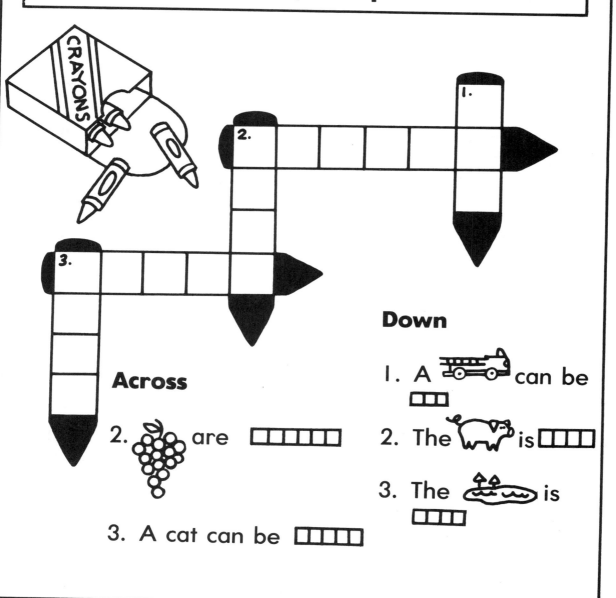

Across

2. 🍇 are ☐☐☐☐☐☐

3. A cat can be ☐☐☐☐☐

Down

1. A 🚒 can be ☐☐☐

2. The 🐷 is ☐☐☐☐

3. The 🌱 is ☐☐☐☐

MY FIRST WORDS

Put an X in the box next to the sentence that tells about each picture.

☐ The boy can fly.

☐ The jet can fly.

☐ This train can go fast.

☐ This car can go fast.

☐ They are in a truck.

☐ They are in a house.

Skill: vocabulary review

MY FIRST WORDS

Read each sentence. Draw a circle around Yes or No.

Will they go out and dig?   Yes   No

Will they ride in the car?   Yes   No

Will they jump in and swim?   Yes   No

Will they run to the bus?   Yes   No

Skill: vocabulary review

MY FIRST WORDS

Match each sentence with the right picture. Write the number in the box. ☐

1. The dog likes to dig.

2. The man will help the girl.

3. The boy can go fast!

4. The woman likes to sing.

5. The girl will fly the jet.

Skill: understanding sentences